Gateless Gatecrashers

Liberation Unleashed

Gateless Gatecrashers:

21 Ordinary People... 21 Extraordinary Awakenings

Ilona Ciunaite and Elena Nezhinsky

LIBERATION UNLEASHED

First edition 2012

ISBN: 978-1470028916

Book design by Arc Manor, LLC

For information, please write to:
markedeternal@gmail.com

www.LiberationUnleashed.com

Ready, vigilant and alive, you are there—at the Gate.

Then comes the guide who had crossed before. She takes your hand or slaps your face, depending on what you need, and guides you through the Gate.

You turn back, and see that there is no Gate, there is no crossing, there is no you.

And there never was.

ARE YOU READY?

Contents

Introduction

by Ilona Ciunaite

There is a simple, obvious truth: there is no such entity as "me". There is no self at all, as in zero. There is only life flowing freely as one reality.

Life just is. It is so simple that we miss it. We don't stop to look at what's always happening.

Because of this omission, each person in this world is born into a prison, and spends their entire life feeding, protecting and trying to build and redeem something that was never there to begin with. This is the engine of all human chaos.

Seeing through this illusion takes seconds—if you're honest, and you know where to look. That's what this book is about.

We are not doing anything; doing is happening. There is no doer, no thinker, no manager that decides what, when, with whom or why. Life just happens, and we have no say in it. There is no us.

The belief that we all have a special separate self which is in charge of our life is nothing but an unquestioned assumption. Human beings see life filtered through this core belief. The feeling of separation persists in everyday experience, making life stressful, dark or threatening. More than anything, it feels incomplete.

Those lucky enough to know that there is a way out, a mysterious thing known as enlightenment, often spent years fruitlessly seeking a truth that is simple, real, and immediate—right in front of their eyes.

If you feel that something is wrong, that there is something to find out, that life is not full, not enough, somehow incomplete—but should be otherwise—this book is for you.

If you are looking for exciting ideas, please look elsewhere. No exciting ideas here, just a hard look at reality. And if you are looking for something to take the responsibility for finding the truth out of your hands—this book is not for you either.

The truth cannot be spoonfed. The only people who ever see the truth, and step through that Gateless Gate are those who decide to take responsibility for finding out what the truth really is.

Liberation has been oversold. It does not guarantee immediate and passive release from suffering, or freedom from thoughts, or love and peace forever. That's a caricature. The reality is different—but it is genuine. Finding that reality for yourself brings clarity—and opens a new path to developing a way of life that is smooth, kind, humble, and overflowing with joy.

The truth is simple. There is no self. There never was.

If you accept this as a belief, without testing, without sincere investigation, nothing will change. You will have one more belief running in the system, creating even more conflicts than before—and although you might find them interesting at first, like all beliefs, they get old fast.

To see the truth of it, you need to look. That means you must leave all expectations, all precious opinions aside and take a fresh, honest look. Don't look for big shining lights, or big insights. Just look for the truth.

Looking is simple: hold a clear intention to finally see the truth, no matter what, watch out for distractions that the mind creates, and keep digging further. It's not scary. It is not magic. Just start looking for yourself and answer some precise questions with honesty. Be honest like you've never been before. Then you'll see how obvious and simple the truth is.

Some call it Liberation, others crossing the Gate, Stream Entry, Self Realisation, Awakening, Enlightenment, Anatta. Whatever name you give it, this is most important realisation in your life. It marks the end of believing and the beginning of seeing things as they are.

Years of conditioning and programming don't disappear immediately. There is a clean-up time, a settling in period that is unique to everybody.

But once something is seen, it cannot be unseen, so life gets a very different flavour. That flavour is the sweet taste of freedom.

It is not the end of suffering; it's seeing that there is no sufferer. And it leads to freedom to experience without the frustrating need to change anything. With frustration and neediness absent, changing what does need to change becomes much more straightforward.

So if you are looking for freedom, this is it. This book contains the full transcripts of 21 guided liberations. Real liberations, real people, in real life. Half of them are people I guided through. The others were guided by my friend, and constant inspiration, Elena.

Nothing has been left out. These transcripts record the full interaction between seeker and guide that ended in these 21 people's awakening. The transcripts are no idle boast. We wrote this book to give you a map, a crystal clear understanding of exactly how to step through the Gate to freedom.

And if you feel that perhaps you are not ready for this freedom?

Gatecrash!

Crossing the Gateless Gate—Are You Ready?

by Elena Nezhinsky

When I was at The Gate, I had no patience left for any more search.

I was burning for truth.

That night somebody guided me to see that for all this time, for years and years, who was searching for whatever goal, holding whatever intention, was an imaginary self.

Years in silent retreats, sitting day after day, staring inside, purifying the mind. Needed at the time, but not anymore.

The search that drove half of my life was suddenly suffocating me. I was ready to cross, to step through, but I didn't know where this path led. In various spiritual books I read about some kind of veil of illusion and The Gateless Gate. I heard this koan many times—had no idea what it meant—until I felt like I was standing there—at The Gate.

You feel it in your bones—standing there with your entire being.

Something really powerful is going on—not even sure what—like burning from inside out with a wish for Truth. It feels ready. This is the time. I must cross. I must rip off this illusion. What the illusion is, not even sure yet, just intellectually maybe, if you have read or heard about it before. But there is a strong feeling, as if you are about to step and fall into an abyss—the abyss of the unknown.

What was before was thoroughly explored. It may have been comfortable, good, great, happy, not so good, disappointing, boring, painful—anything—but at least it's familiar.

Fear comes, in some cases even terror.

It feels that death is here—the death of the old life.
The death of the illusion.

Hesitation comes.

Then the decision: turn back to the familiar or forward into the unknown?

The decision comes.

Ready, vigilant and alive, you are there—at the Gate.

Then comes the guide who had crossed before. She takes your hand or slaps your face, depending on what you need, and guides you through the Gate.

You turn back, and see that there is no Gate, there is no crossing, there is no you.

And there never was.

ARE YOU READY?

Philip

For Philip it was really intense. He had suffered a lot, big fear, panic attacks, frustration and burning desire for truth. But I was surprised how quickly he saw through fear, and after that it became possible to go further. He got stuck at the me-ness, as he called it, and after looking at it as the glue that holds the illusion together, he finally gave up and then all was over. I was really happy to help Philip ease the suffering that comes with belief in separate self.—I. C.

Philip: Dear Ilona,

I love reading the conversational posts on your blog. You come across as very patient and understanding, yet don't allow any bullshit to slip by.

I'm a fifty-five-year old man living in Australia and I have been inquiring into this for many years and have a great deal of conceptual understanding of the illusion of self. Yet I have not seen it directly. Do you think that, possibly, some like myself are just simply unable go beyond that point?

Ilona: No. I don't think that's possible. It is possible that the wall of knowing is so thick that simple things are not visible. Once looking starts, it is simple, but to get to that point one needs to be ready to look at everything with fresh eyes.

Are you ready? I can help.

Philip: Thanks for that, Ilona. It would be great if I could get some help.

At times I think so deeply about this that my mind seems to seek revenge; it wakes me up at 2am with thoughts of unsolvable puzzles which trigger panic attacks.

During the waking hours I have been meditating on the notion that everything is as it should be and could not be any other way, so I should give up any resistance to what is and go along with whatever comes up, even the panic thoughts.

This does work to a degree, but not to shift anything in a lasting way, maybe it is just another theory or technique? Anxiety about what may happen in the future dominates most of my thinking and as you say it seems very thick and strong. Simple seeing seems very elusive.

Ilona: No, it's not just another theory or technique. This is a one-off seeing and you're done. What is seen cannot be unseen, just as once you see that Santa isn't real, you can never un-see that!

You don't have to look at the empty fireplace where Santa should be, until something magic happens and the belief magically dissolves. Someone just suggests it to you, or says it to you—there is no Father Christmas.

Then you look around. And you think. You think for yourself. And very quickly it becomes obvious that—oh my God—everything fits. All the contradictions about Santa, questions about Santa. Issues about Santa. They are what fall away.

This is exactly the same as seeing that there is no self. Because it's just one more fiction. In and of itself, the fiction of 'you' is just one more fiction. Yes, it's fundamental to a lot of destructive patterns, behaviour, and human dysfunction. One might argue that it's fundamental to all human dysfunction. But in and of itself? It's just one more fiction. And you just see through it like you'd see through any fiction.

It's not about fighting resistance, it's about clearing up crap inside that clashes and creates that resistance. We are not looking here for new beliefs, but for a simple truth. And as the man said, the truth will set you free.

What I want you to do is answer me with 100% honesty, and then only when the answer feels right. No rush, but when I ask you to look, really look.

So now look at the real possibility that there is no "you" in real life. That all is happening by itself, without a manager. Look inside and tell me what feeling comes up; do you recognise fear, resistance, frustration, what is it?

Describe what you see.

Philip: When I consider the possibility that there is no "me", there is a great fear and sadness that arises, a feeling that I will lose my family and all that I have become.

It seems far too unknown to give into; what if I accept this and go mad? Maybe I don't trust that it will deliver. I understand that there is no control really, but that understanding does nothing to reduce the fear of uncertainty. I really don't know what truth is. Is this true all this exists?

Ilona: Of course this looks scary and sad—you think you stand to lose something by seeing this. But what is lost? What can be lost? There's nothing there to lose. Let it be OK. It's just fear; your family is fine and nothing will be lost.

Now look at that fear. Can you see that this is a mechanism of protection, that this fear is hiding something from being found out? Can you notice how perfectly it does its job? Can you respect and honour that mechanism?

Now look at it and just let the fear be, without fighting it. Now look behind it. What is behind? What do you see?

Philip: Yes! Yes! I can see how tenacious the fear is. As you say, it seems to be protecting something and constantly testing my resolve. The fear is very efficient, yes. At times it is so overwhelming and debilitating.

But wow, reading that, I had a glimpse of the behind and I started laughing out loud. This was in the architect's office where I work; so strange to have that moment in such a stiff, uptight environment. I will write some more tonight.

Ilona: Great! Yes, please write more tonight. Answer this: what needs to be protected?

Dig more here.

Philip: My life as I know it needs protection.

This sense of me in the world seems like a delicate balance of good and bad. I can see the absurdity of that because it just causes so much misery when things go more to the bad, but it's like I'm right in it.

It seems impossible to see a way out without everything crashing or me going mad. The glimpses I get are only that, and the whole thing rolls back in again. When you asked what was behind the fear, I felt a very calm sense of peace, like a clear sky behind a dark dust cloud, and it seemed so obvious that I laughed.

Yet I feel great frustration at not really seeing this fully. Then I ask who or what is frustrated, is it me who is frustrated? Who is seeing the frustration?

Ilona, you blow me away, you don't know me from Adam yet you take the time for this. Why? I mean, don't get me wrong, it is truly wonderful, but no one I know would do this—not even my therapist or my wife. It's amazing!

Ilona: It's a great start we are having here—you busted through the fear in no time. Yes, behind the fear is nothing, the peaceful silent nothing and yet it makes so much fuss in human lives.

We will go through this step by step and at the end it will all become clear. Trust that. The process has started. Now you just need to notice that it is happening already. All by itself.

I'll help you with the frustration. No one is feeling, seeing or owning it. You can look and go mad and never find it. Just do the same as with fear, look right at frustration, look at the friction of beliefs and burning for the truth. It's there, showing the way forward. Just a feeling that rises up. Feelings come and go like thoughts, notice that and just let them be there.

Now I want you to look at the real possibility that there is no manager in life at all. What comes up? Thoughts, feelings—just examine everything and look at what else is there.

Why I do this? There is no gift greater than man's freedom. It is an amazing thing to be able to give this to people. Really. And the feeling of guiding someone to freedom and seeing them break free—what price could you put on that? Believe me—I am rewarded.

The battle in the head will dissolve once we look at it, for now don't fight the content, but look at what is going on in there: thoughts racing, charged with emotions. All this is effortless. Can you see?

Philip: Frustration. There is tension in that I sense I am very close, I can smell the freedom, yet... can't even say what it is. All the knowing is done. Is it courage?

Ilona: Frustration is good at this time. Just go with it, let it be there. Notice that it's a feeling plus a labelling by the mind. What do you mean by "all knowing is done"?

Carry on, Philip. What is it?

Philip: It is lightness of being. I have this lightness pervading everything. It's like the heaviness is lifting from the body. The 'knowing' that is done, what I meant is that I don't feel the need at the moment to read any more Tolle etc. which I have in the past.

I have this sense of something falling away and, as you say, just letting it all happen. I'm not in control, how could I be? It just appears that way, but that is OK for the character Phil because that is his nature, his appearance, just appearing and seeing that appearance. Cool! Sorry I am unable to write more at the moment; will continue later.

Ilona: Hi Philip. How is it going? Are you through?

Philip: Yeah! I can see the possibility, yet there is great deception and dishonesty. As much as I want so much to directly see this (do I?) the fear is doing a great job, as well as wanting to please you, because you have transcended this, which is more "me", I know.

I could write a paper on this, yet there is nothing shifting, nothing direct. Mind on mind on mind tricks. Fuck it! Years of crusty protection, how do you break through that? At times it seems like a great chasm. I want to be honest, yet when I wake up in sweat at one in the morning there is nothing to hold on to. Help!

Even the writing of this is being criticised by a voice in my head as being useless at times; it really is a battle going on in there. I will write some more, later in the day.

Ilona: You cannot see this, as there is no "you". There is only seeing happening. The seen, the seer and the seeing are one and the same.

Fear is just a mechanism that protects the illusion from being found out. It is doing a great job, but if you look behind it, you'll see that there is nothing there, nothing that needs to be protected.

You don't need to understand everything about the wall in order to demolish it, right? You just hammer it through. You do it by looking at the protection itself. How does it work, what does it do? What do you see here?

No, there is nothing to hold on. Everything you think you know is useless here. Because there is no one there that needs to hold on, only thoughts arising: "it's scary, there's nothing to hold on."

Who is thinking these thoughts? Or maybe they are just passing by as a result of the clash of different beliefs?

Another way through? Think of this—you see the frustration and the knowledge as these barriers? Whose frustration? Whose knowledge? Who owns this frustration? This knowledge? The point is not to beat it down. The point is—it's not attached to anything. It's just hanging there, feeding itself, and claiming to belong to 'you'. But there is no you.

Investigate that. Who is thinking? What is behind thinking? What influences thoughts?

Thought does not think. Is this true?

Philip: Hey. Yes, something more direct. During a panic attack at 4am, I saw that it was just this dense ball of thought begging to be acknowledged, and the beginnings of the wall of fear.

For the first time, I had the clarity to see it for what it was, just another dense black cloud passing through, not belonging to anyone.

There is no ownership; ownership brings the burden of maintaining something. I sensed that the control I was so desperate for was not possible or necessary. When I gave it up, it's like the grip of fear was diminished, and it wasn't mine, just fear. It's like the opening I have been looking for, the gate. Beyond that black cloud I could sense the clear sky. The sweet, sweet taste. I feel like I can push it more.

Ilona: But who/what is there to push? Is it not all just happening by itself? The unfolding, the manifestation of life in every moment?

Experience plus labelling by the mind is also part of everything.

All is happening without control. Is this true, that there is no "I" to experience, that "I" is just a thought that passes by just like that cloud of fear, without control? A thought preceding other thoughts. And thought does not think.

Who is sensing, or is it just sense of freedom appearing in awareness? Come on! Now it's soooo close!

Philip: The "I" is an assumed identity referring to some centre or personal source, my source. It's full of me-ness, precious me-ness. The organism has unity but it has no centre.

The whole centre thing is impossible; where did it come from, how could you think that? It's all part of a whole organism, all interrelated. There is still this sense of absence, like a hollow emptiness that is both frightening and beautiful. There is letting be, but letting be by whom?

Does there need to be a doer, or is there just doing? Each time the mind needs to refer to an author and doer, the "I" has come in, yet that is also seen. Each seeing emanates that sense of relief. It's more than that, but I don't have the words.

Like I said before, all I can say is that it is a sweetness, a sweet sweetness. I can't seem to talk to others about this. It always sounds so clumsy and comes out like an awkward philosophy. So I don't.

There is no thinking about and no doing, just seeing and the me-ness makes no sense. It seems to need that support. Things, as you say, look after themselves. The brain drives the car very well, it even designs the house, and the "me" seems to come in later to want to make sense of it.

Really very funny when it is seen. The world is so full of "my this" and "my that", it's hilarious.

Ilona: I had to read what you wrote three times to get what you are saying. Yes it is difficult to express in words. But I see you are starting to see!

Remember the Matrix movie, when Neo gets out and he looks around and says "why do my eyes hurt", and the answer comes, "you've never used them before"...

So it is with creatively and originally describing things that you see with your own eyes.

Our culture creates this web of pre-packaged thought and ways of speaking. Spirituality is no different. Conventions. Set conventions of thinking and putting sentences together. When you look at life with fresh eyes, and have to find your own words to describe what you see.

Sweetness. I like this word.

"Me-ness", define that, please. Can you look a bit more here, what is that? And what is Philip?

Philip: Thank you for being so patient. The me-ness is the concern for the fictitious "I".

It's like, say, taking offence at being insulted when someone judges or criticises you, or reacts to what you said as being "stupid". The character "Philip" has learned to defend the me-ness. But what is the me-ness except just this construct of the story of the person "Philip"?

Yet the person, the me-ness, seems to have this mind of its own, it reacts and comes up with offence no matter what. That is the frustration. I can see all this but it still goes on. Is this just the process of dismantling or am I missing something?

Ilona: If I have this right, your word "me-ness" is the glue that holds illusion together. How is that glue these days, still strong and sticky or is it getting looser?

Philip: Yeah! Nice, the glue is brittle and falling away as we speak, like old resin. When I see this it reminds me of when I was a child; a very familiar sense and an "of course" moment.

It's as if I had been lost in this wilderness for fifty years and just managed to emerge from the darkness, but it's like something I knew all along. It's very familiar. The character "Philip" still seems a bit lost and bewildered at having to be in the world.

Ilona: It's OK, Philip is fine. Just that huge chunk of belief has been knocked out, so he needs a bit of time to rebalance. Conditioning will keep falling off for a while, depending on how many beliefs are stored in the system.

To help this process along, you can look at the most precious beliefs closest to your heart. Just examine what is there, identify and release.

So, what is real? Is there a self in any shape or form in reality?

Philip: Life is profoundly empty and meaningless and what a relief.

Ultimately, there is nothing in the "this". It's like the present is paper-thin but really nothing; it has no dimension. The brain fleshes it out to give the whole thing dimension and to make sense of it in terms of this separate me.

The brain has learned so much about being in the world and still conducts processes with that knowledge. But hey, the difference is it's not doing it for anyone, it's just doing it. There is no need for someone to control things and make decisions.

In fact, that would not be possible. There is no control; life is in free fall. It's just that somehow, somewhere along the line, something assumed ownership of intent and outcome, as you say it's all on automatic.

The strictures of this assumption are so obvious and profoundly different, it's like being anally retentive your whole life, the sphincter muscle holding it all in, trying to control the uncontrollable for all those years and for what? Limitation. Fresh and new, my tinnitus stopped for the first time this morning in twenty years, just silence, sweet...

Belief... Philip believes in goodness and integrity, in the love of his family and doing his best. All OK, but just tasks mapped out within a limited perspective. It's so utterly obvious the world seems mad inside this totally unnecessary limitation.

I was reminded of that song by Del Amitri, "when you're driving with your brakes on, when you're swimming with your boots on".

Thank you, sweet Ilona, in the emptiness you helped me see.

Ilona: Look—reality is very real. Things are real. People are real. It's just that nothing owns them.

Now you're free, don't fall into the trap of disconnecting from all reality. That's just a dogma of pop spirituality, it isn't what's needed, or best. What's best is the opposite—to get a clearer, and cleaner, and truer sense of things, because the life that's happening responds with brilliance, and originality to life seen clearly.

You are most welcome, Philip. I'm so glad you looked and saw it. Thank you so much. And welcome to living free.

Shane

Helping Shane was an honour. He is an ordained Buddhist minister and meditation teacher. He wrote to me after reading my work with Professor Waldo. Shane is a very humble man, and extremely open about this work with me. He feels that combining the traditional meditation path with direct pointing will help many practitioners to realise Anatta*—no-self. He is now helping his students with classical meditation instructions and direct pointing.—E. N.*

Shane: Hello, Elena.

Thank you for your willingness to look at this. I admire and respect your dedication toward helping others.

A little about my background. I have been practising meditation consistently for over fifteen years and have been teaching meditation and Buddhist principles for seven of those. I am an ordained Buddhist minister, but shy away from the ritualistic practices of Buddhism. I teach three or four times per week to help people find a solution to ease their troubles.

I have literally gone through hundreds and hundreds of meditation students. I have written several books on the subject, and lead by example by practising sitting meditation a lot! But! No one, to my knowledge, is waking up! There is no permanent liberation to be found. Nobody, including myself, is getting truly free.

In my personal practice I have seen improvements in clarity and understanding of selflessness. I have a love for the truth. That is what motivates me. I have the determination to look inside and see what is not there. There are moments of seeing through the illusion, but it does not stick.

There is this self-talk that says "this is a gradual path, just relax and it will come" and then there is the other inner voice that says "you don't have much time, get this done with, see through the illusion of the 'I' NOW and for ever and really help others."

I enjoy teaching, but even more, there is the inner drive to help people through their suffering. You have this same drive. I understand that the suffering that is so prevalent in the people I meet is from the false identity of "self". Although to truly liberate others, I should first be free from this illusion myself, otherwise it seems like I am teaching people what I know and that seems to be how to relax the body and still the mind.

I am needing a push. I know it is possible get beyond this wall. I wish to see the truth and have it last and stick. I want to hear that SNAP in the back of the head and know that I really qualify to talk to others about what their life can be like once liberated. I know that what you and the others are doing here works, and see it as THE opportunity of lifetimes.

Elena: I appreciate your honesty, Shawn. This what will get you through: being willing to re-examine your immediate experience of what is what. So let's just do that. Look at "I" right now and tell me what you see. One by one, anything that arises—write.

Shane: When looked at, "I" seems to arise and fall away. Such as, when something has to be done or when a mind state is noticed, it seems to be more present. Just now, when searching for a way to communicate this, the "I" did not seem to be present. So there seems to be a strong "I should do this" or "I will be doing" or "I did that". But it does seem to come and go. Oh!

One strong thing I just realised, is that when I noticed that you called me Shawn instead of Shane, a sense of shaken identity or a grasping at the "I" arose.

Elena: Yes, the Shawn/Shane thing. I did that on purpose.

That's a fib.

It's strong, this grasping. I called Robert S. "Bob" and the same thing happened! Look how the label "Shane" is just the same as label "I". It's just a label.

What is Shane? A word/thought + emotions + sensations.
What is "I"? A word/thoughts + emotions + sensations.

Thought—exists.
Emotions—exist.
Sensations—exist.

Shawn—just a label.
I—just a label.

Do not take this as a belief. Take it as a clue. A clue to investigate in a certain direction. Ok?

Let me know what comes up.

Shane: It is noticed right away that what comes up is a feeling of tension or uneasiness. The label is just there. Thought triggers emotion and sensation; the result is this uneasiness.

Elena: Shane is a label, as is Shawn too! So we have this feeling arising when the label is a little off. You are the Theravada guy; you can break up the experience and see:

- Feelings—yes.
- Uncomfortable sensations—yes.
- Associated thoughts—yes.

"Me"?—no.

Where is the self in all of that?

Sense of self—yes.

Actual self—no.

But again, you can look deeply at what the sense of self is: all the same thoughts, sensations, feelings.

Please look at all this, and write to me what's going on.

You are very close, can't be otherwise with all your experience...
... which is not yours. It just is.

Experience is. The thought "I", "mine", comes and claims the experience.

Sharing is just happening, you know. Are you doing it? No. You know it's just a movement that gets expressed in a particular way. So why should anything else be different?

Ask yourself, ask where you hang on. What is that? Please do not go into equanimity, go hot and desperate and ask. "Where the hell am I clinging?!"

ASK! INVESTIGATE!

Shane: There is a strong feeling that staying with the immediate experience is key here. This being the only reality there is.

The only place where we can find true honesty in any situation. So, with the arising of a thought, there seems to be the co-arising or the manipulation of the already present emotions and sensations. This can sound deeper than it really is, can't it?

It is just what it is. These things happen and they are not me as long as I do not try to attach a story to all of it. It occurs to me that even when attaching a story to these arising things, it still is not the truth. Just a false label that is applied to the process of thought-emotions-sensations or as you said, what is what.

Elena: What you wrote to me was more like a discourse, Shane.

We both don't need that, really.

Let's do this. I will push, you look, and come back and answer EXACTLY what was asked. You try your best not to analyse, otherwise I will have to slap you, Shane.

Even though I do respect all your experience, at the same time, I would not be doing what I am doing if I just listened to you. I trust what's arising here, so if I read and I feel no interest, no concentration in what you wrote to me, I trust that.

Was it great insight? Maybe, but I don't care. Keep a very narrow focus, and won't step even one step sideways. Tell me if it this is OK with you, and if you are willing to stay to the end? And if you are willing to stop reading no-self, non-duality stuff while with me, if you are willing to have raw emotions, and if you are willing to look at them in the way I ask you.

I am going to wait for your answer.

Shane: Yes, Elena, let's do this. No reading stuff and raw emotions. I read your question as "Where the hell am I clinging?!" So I am just going to just write here... this is tough because I feel as if there is something that I should be fighting off, like beating down with a stick to get rid of it, but don't know what it is for sure.

Elena: You did not answer my question, Shane. Here it is again: "ask yourself, ask where you hang on. What is that? Please do not go into equanimity, go hot and desperate and ask. "Where the hell am I clinging?!" ASK."

Shane: To the attempt to be that intelligent, charming, funny, nice, hard working guy. But I wonder what all of that is. Is it the "I" or is it just the way I see the personality or want to? Seems strange, but I seem to be looking for something to let go of, something bad or wrong, and find it frustrating not knowing what it is.

Elena: That's WHY you're clinging. Not what I asked. WHAT are you clinging TO?

Here's how it goes with Theravada people: they focus their attention, divide the experience, look, understand, etc. What's wrong with this? The self that is in the middle of each step.

You came to me and said: I feel this dissatisfaction, I feel the search is still going, I have a burning desire to see the truth to help others. It is very noble intention, very cool. And it's great you know it is possible. It means that it is possible for you. Any moment.

So when I tell you to ask yourself where you hang on, here is what you do:

You understand that this is essential for you to see the truth. With that understanding and strong intention, to the point of desperation, like this is the last question of your life—only one and then you die—you ASK.

Then you become very quiet, in other words shut up the habitual thinking, analysing, any meditation—whatever you are doing. Completely shut it off. And listen.

"The clinging could be..."

So I won't hear "could be" or "should be"—it must be clear seeing.

Let's do it again.

Shane: I did just as you asked... it is being! It is continually trying to be something or someone. A relentless trying to be this or that. A teacher, an author, a humanitarian, whatever... it is being. NOT to let it be... but to be somebody.

I will have to let this settle to see if there is something more. But there are tears...

Elena: So now look plainly, physically, with two eyes, and see that beingness is going on, regardless of you trying to be, tensing in this "somebody" or that one… it just is.

And tensing/contracting is that beingness too. There is no "you". Regardless of how beingness presents itself.

No "you". There are labels that claim something is 'yours' or whatever, yes.

Actual "you?"—not at all. Nada.

See that this beingness does not require you as an entity there to manage its flow. Look at a baby. When a baby is born there is only being, beingness there. The baby is one with its environment. It cries out of sensations of hunger; movement happens toward the breast. Where is self in all that?

Nowhere. Something happens later when the baby starts to associate the sensations and the body with himself—"I", "mine". All experience now is divided and labelled. But what's the truth?

There is no separation, no entity. So all your life now this paradox is trying to resolve itself. This is the suffering—the turmoil of dissatisfaction, of seeking, of feeling incomplete, of the feeling of something missing. That's where it comes from. That's what's driving it. That, that only.

And you can meditate, you can analyze, you can think deep thoughts, but until the label is seen again as a label, this will continue.

The owner was never there, it was always just an illusion. Take the interest and the time to mount a genuine investigation into this simple statement. Find the truth of it. Can you look now and tell me what you see? Look right at your experience.

What is there?

Shane: The experience right now! Is that there is the world being the world with its sounds and colours. Sense information coming into this body. Everything is happening as it should. No surprises. When just sitting here seeing and looking at this, It feels like there is no one pushing. Just looking is happening.

Elena: Great. Look now. Answer me this:

Is there a "you" in any shape or form in reality?

Shane: I looked and looked... there is a body, like flesh and bones. But no owner of this stuff.

Elena: Do you exist?

Shane: No, there isn't anything existing. Nothing there to claim its existence. Funny... nothing there to even claim it doesn't exist.

Elena: That. That's it. Look. See the simple truth of it. Again, what is the self?

Shane: It's just a label, really a mistake. Like seeing a shadow and thinking it's real, but with nothing to see. Okay, like thinking of a shadow and believing it's real.

Elena: What is happening now? Tell me, what do you see? What is actually real?

Shane: There is just seeing, thoughts are happening, the body is being the body, there are sounds, and actually very pleasant emotions coming from the not being or not having to be that was mentioned earlier. The body is just sitting and mostly just simply doing.

Elena: OK, great, my friend Shane. And now—chop that wood: lead the classes, wash the dishes, write a book!

Shane: A very joyful Thank you! Thank you! Thank you! You are wonderful, like magic. Your words cut through the crap and into the heart of it.

Things are very clear now! If you need anything, please let me know. And please keep doing this work, it just might be our only hope.

Bruno

I have been friends with Bruno for a while and he used to come to me with some questions from time to time. It was great to see him really getting interested in having a look for himself. He is so full of love and is helping people to work with feelings. It was a great pleasure to help him awaken.—I. C.

Ilona: Hi Bruno. I experienced the shift recently. Yes, I really want to help people free. Quite a few people find me for that. It just feels like the most logical thing to do. Now that I'm settled and the feeling of falling has faded, I find that seeing no self is the key to a more relaxed, peaceful way of life. So I do fight the lie still. But more in a settled way, dissolving rather than attacking it.

There's nothing more to see than what it IS.

Bruno: "There's nothing more to see than what it IS." So from your point of view, you feel that Bruno is free? Do you feel, from my descriptions of what I see, through the lens of no-self, that I'm totally free from the illusion of self?

OK, I guess that these questions are from the linear mind of Bruno, trying to rationalise and process something that is just life flowing... I can see that!

OK, I "need" some guidance. (And yes, illusion again… isn't life amazing?)

Ilona: Everyone is free; most just don't know it yet. You either see it or you don't. Once it's done, that which can fall into illusion is no more.

So can you just tell me, with complete honesty, if you see it clearly or not? If not, we can look at it together. If yes, then there is definite certainty.

Bruno: Thank you for taking time to answer. I really don't want to waste your precious time. So, I decided to really look, to spend time in nature and observe crowds of people to see how Bruno reacts to it—from a perspective totally detached from my character.

The first thing I saw and felt was emptiness mixed with gratitude. I noticed that Bruno's body becomes calm and peaceful. I saw him as if I had separated from the body; like watching it on the screen of a cinema. But then I felt frustrated with a "bad" emptiness. I spent this day really looking and I honestly have to say that I don't see it clearly. I guess "my" problem is trying too much to see the truth...

Ohhh, Ilona, I really want to break free from the illusion of self. Now, I feel confused, frustrated and angry—and I know that these are good tools to set me free...

Guide me, please!

Ilona: My time is not more precious than your freedom.

Looks like you are ready. So here it comes. Your problem is obvious. You think that you need to see something that you do not see yet. This feels real to you. But, since there is no "you" in reality, "you" cannot see it. "I" is a thought. It points to nothing.

Let's look at the thought itself. What is it, where does it come from? Can you control thoughts, stop them?

"I" is a thought that precedes other thoughts when mind labels experience. It comes with language.

I breathe—rather than "breathing is happening". I walk—rather than "walking is happening". I digest—"digesting is happening". I observe—"observing is happening".

The mind labels experience. That is its job. But you don't have to believe thoughts, do you? You can look at a thought, look at reality, and see the difference. The confusion is in the mind, reality is. There's nothing else to see than what's going on already.

Look, what is "university"? Is there such a thing in reality or is it just a label to point to buildings, students, books, all things that are real? But there is no university. Just a label.

"I" is a label for 'the thing that owns the life that's being lived'. So that "I" is just a thought. A label.

"I" is not looking. Looking is happening at this moment. It is happening by itself without the need for a self to look. Notice the obvious. What do you see?

Bruno: I see that thoughts come from nowhere. Constantly making pop-ups, without the intervention of any self. If "I" try to stop them, new thoughts instantly emerge to destroy the belief that I am the creator; that it's me who has the power to create them and destroy them.

Today, the observing happens in very different way... The thought emerged along with emotions and the observations just happened, without any self. There wasn't any idea that I am that. Basically, they appeared and left as fast as they arrived. I just let it go.

Yes, I totally understand that the self is just a label. Just like the analogy of the university—excellent example, by the way! The "I" does not look. Yes, no one is looking. Only the looking manifesting itself, through a physical body. Life is observing itself!

I see that there is no one suffering. Just thoughts about a character that is suffering, just like in a movie. We sympathise with the character that appears in the thoughts and then, we assume (with another thought) that we are inside the story. And therefore we fall into the illusion that we exist!

Ilona: Keep going. What is "I"?

Bruno: The self is an illusory identity. It is a label that has been impressed on us since childhood, precisely at the age when we mimic the adults. It is a program that was assumed by the mind as a way to control and ensure survival in the society we are located in. It is a mechanism apprehended by the mind. "I" is a concept that was delivered to us. Unlike life: when we are born, we are born with life! On the other hand, the "I" was given to us by the social environment.

Ilona: Cool; you are seeing it! Is there a definite certainty or is there is a doubt? What happened? What made you see? Is there a "you" there in any shape or form?

Bruno: Just like the knowledge that is given to us at school, Self is given to us, mandatorily, so it is recorded in memory, without having the chance to question what we have been given. This is how thousands of generations have acquired knowledge, without being able to question the authority of those who gave us the self.

I cannot detect any doubt. Something changed... but I cannot explain why... I cannot describe this experience that is manifesting. I wonder if it is true that there is no "me"? No answer, just silence. Just a feeling of lightness. A smile.

I will write to you tomorrow with what I see. For now, I want to see it better, enjoy what it IS. So strange... but in a good way! So smooth... (This is what is happening right now)

Ilona: Morning! How is the view today?

Can you tell me: What is Bruno? What is real?

Bruno: You asked: "What is Bruno?"

I could answer, "it is a character". But the truth is that when I put that question to myself, the first thing that comes up is nothing. I really don't know who Bruno is. And, to tell the truth, I do not need to have an answer.

Everything is right. The mind is calm for the first time in the life of the character Bruno. Nothing has changed and everything has changed. How to explain the unexplainable? Life remains the same. The same everyday challenges, the same thoughts arise, the same emotions arise... Everything is the same but at the same time, everything has changed.

The truth is that despite all the problems (challenges) that arise, such as a terrible toothache arising because of the wisdom tooth that is emerging, the mind is calm. I observe and I'm mindlessly in peace. "How interesting this pain is. Life expressing itself..." I say to myself.

Some debts to pay and deadlines approaching and I see that everything is all right. No drama. As soon as the thought that I am fucked comes, I notice that it's just a thought, which is an illusion. And peace appears in the body. The feeling of guilt that Bruno had over not working harder, for not acting more quickly, has vanished.

Sometimes a feeling of irritation arises, caused by something external. I observe and let it go! Simple!

I look at the trees that I see every day when I walk in nature and although they are the same, now I see life in them! It's so weird, Ilona. But at the same time perfect! A feeling that makes me shiver, of such perfection, and it's obvious that it's what I'm seeing!

The trees are exactly the same, but the landscape has changed in some way! So much life is flowing. How come I never saw it before? It's right there. It's always been there, in front of me! What perfection—the word comes out of my mouth. And Bruno is not there to interfere in anything.

Ilona: Bruno, my friend, welcome to the flow. I'm delighted for you.

Thank you for looking.

With love,
Ilona.

Bruno: Thank you so much for guiding me, Ilona! Thank you for your dedication to showing the truth to others! Thank you for your kindness and your wisdom! When I first read all the posts on your blog, I knew that the truth was real! I immediately felt empathy with you!

I have to thank life for showing me your presence! And please continue showing the truth to others! And I'm here if you need anything!

Jamie

Jamie is, to date, the funniest guy I've met doing this work. This conversation is hilarious. When he wrote to me, I felt that he already saw that self does not exist, but did not believe the experience, so I hit him pretty hard. Hang on to your hat...—E. N.

Jamie: Hi, Elena.

I wonder if you could help me with this "there's no me" stuff, please? I've been following your blog for some time now, and everything rings true—except I can't see it, I feel I'm stuck.

When I look for a self I never find anything, and never have. For at least two decades I've been avoiding social contact because I felt it was dishonest to pretend I was there when in reality I wasn't, so I would isolate myself until such times that I felt I could muster an "I" to present. This probably sounds like crap, but do you follow me?

When I say I'm stuck it's because I seem to understand all this at least conceptually, and I also cannot find any self when I look for one. However, somehow I still think I exist, and I can't seem to get through that barrier.

Do you have time to help me?

Elena: Of course.

You can't find something that does not exist. Agreed? Can you find a unicorn in your room? Do you even go and look for it when I ask you?

So why are you still looking for the self? There's nothing there to find. But here—this is subtle—if you keep looking, hoping that you'll finally 'get' it?

You're waiting for your self to get it. Right?

It's not about staring at the absence, slack-jawed, until the magic happens. It's seeing the shape of reality. That life is, was, and always will be, uncaused. It's just flowing. Right?

Investigate that. Is that true?

Jamie: I cannot see myself, no matter what direction I look in, but it seems there's an implicit assumption that I must be somewhere—if not, who else is experiencing all this? When I investigate that assumption, I find that "I" can be anything, so to speak. I look and find a tension in my throat or abdomen. Before I looked, I thought it was me.

After I look, I find it's just a tension or a sensation (e.g. the feeling of my bottom sitting on the chair). Or even a sound outside the house. When I don't check the assumption I think the sound is me, after I check I see that it's just a sound.

It's like "it" will find anything—a sound, a sensation, a thought—and claim ownership, say "it's me". When I look at it to see if it's true it "dissolves" or "evaporates", but it will just find something else to attach itself to. It seems like an endless chain of events: every time it is revealed that it/this is not me, it will just jump to something else, and it seems I'm too lazy or tired to keep following it.

I guess I'm stuck here…

Elena: Trust experience. You are looking for some improvements in your life. Guess what? There was never a "you". Always just Life living. You saw—yep, no me, just a label. What's there? Life. Just living.

There's no you living it. And it's not about agreeing with that, or living in isolation because you believe this makes everything a lie.

Everything isn't a lie, Jamie. Life is real. It's just not owned.

Now stop being weird. Go outside, walk and look around how Life is living and doesn't need a manager.

Go and walk and look with your two physical eyes, look with wonder, like a kid.

And write what you find. Precise, no fluff.

Jamie: OK, here's what I found out:

When I walk outside there's a field of view. Objects—be it humans, dogs, trees, cars—appear into and disappear from this field of view. This field of view appears in a bigger "view" or space that contains everything that can be sensed: sight, hearing, sensations, smells, tastes, thoughts (text or picture), feelings.

Everything seems to appear from "out of the blue" in this space—much like a car that suddenly emerge into daylight from an unlit tunnel—and it also dissolves back into this space after some time.

In this big space I find no trace of myself. However, there's a very strong tendency to either put the label "me" on some of these objects or to think that I am the source of these objects. Bodily sensations mostly belong to the first type (e.g., the sensations of my feet as I walk on the pavement) whereas thoughts etc. mostly belong to the second type.

When I came back home I watched a movie and tried to find out who is watching. There's definitely sight/seeing, but when I look for the seer I cannot find him. The same with music: There's definitely hearing, but I cannot locate a hearer. It just seems to happen.

But at the same time there's a pervasive "There must be a seer/hearer, keep looking!"—not in words, not in pictures, more like a very strong assumption with an implicit "You shouldn't even challenge this!" attached. It must be a thought since it's in the mind, so to speak, but it doesn't quite look like the usual thoughts.

Eating a Wasa cracker with butter and cheese is such a pleasant experience: the sound of chewing the crisp bread, the feeling of the soft and cold cheese against the lips and the palate. The slight burnt taste of the cracker and the, well, cheesy taste of cheese. I can find no smeller, taster, etc. in this experience.

If I have to be honest, I have to say that it is just happening. But there's a very, very strong tendency to slap a "me" label on the whole thing. It's utterly confusing. The intellect says it's the same as saying "I can clearly see there's no unicorn in this room, but keep looking—there's gotta be one somewhere!" Still, it's like the thought is struggling with reality. How can I get out of this?

Elena: Stop acting like a child, Jamie. There is no "you". It is just a label to the experience. Look at reality, find the truth if this. Stop hiding behind your ideas. You either see it or not.

Is there any "you" in reality in any shape or form?

Find out. Now. Answer me.

Jamie: No, there is no "me" in reality in any shape or form.

There is the whole world, and there are thoughts and feelings, but I am nowhere to be found. If anything, the label "I" is slapped on every goddamn thing there is—be it a sensation, a thought or an emotion—but "I" as an entity is non-existent.

Elena: Awesome. I want to ask you what changed since we spoke. Seems like you got the simplicity of it. No expectations anymore. Good.

Liberation is simple. Illusion is complicated.

Jamie: Elena, nothing has changed, except... I realised I would be lying if I told you there was an "I", and you wanted the truth.

But, Elena, this can't be it, can it? Please don't tell me that THIS is what I've been looking for!? I have a whole library with books that claim to be able to get me enlightened (what a shitty word!), and I've been meditating my ass off for 25 years.

For THIS?! It's gotta be a joke! I don't know whether I should laugh or cry. LOL! If anything, those books have kept me unenlightened! And instead of meditating I could've taken a nap. I've unwittingly deprived myself from sleep for 25 years because I wanted to wake up. Dammit. Do I feel really stupid now?

I want to fuck Jeff Foster! He looks like such a sweet guy, and I absolutely adore his English accent, and I'm sure he'll be good at telling bed time stories—or he could be a stand-up comedian (oh, I forgot, he already is!).

I want to fuck Adyashanti, too. Mostly for taking such a stupid name, but also for his calm and sweet voice. You could think he has developed those manners just to seduce people.

Ok, so I probably won't go and fuck them, I just needed to vent my frustration/anger/what the fuck... No need for anyone out there to feel unsafe, I'm perfectly harmless, hehe.

Although I don't understand why Jed McKenna had to write three fucking books about this, I now understand why he wrote "THIS is NOT what you want!" He's right, this is NOT what I've been looking for, and for the past 25 years I've also been walking in the wrong direction—blindfolded! Jesus!

Nothing has changed, it's always been like this, and I've been trying to prevent it, been jumping through hoops to avoid it. I've been scared like hell. For what? For THIS?! Now I understand "the gateless gate". I've been walking for 25 years to reach that fucking gate, and now that I turn around I see that there has never been any gate to reach—and much less to go through.

Darn...!

Elena: Get some sleep. In fact, take some time in general. Take a few weeks if you need it.

It can be very jarring, to see how small and simple the truth is, in and of itself—especially if you've been searching for 25 years. So many teachers, so many paintings of this amazing place. And then you actually see what the truth is, and... hmmm. Not quite the bells and angels we were led to expect.

But it is real. That matters. And more than this—you hit the nail perfectly on the head when you said "this is this beginning." And it is.

Because even though deep peace doesn't just land in your lap—it will come, over time, as this deepens. It's something to explore, and cultivate.

Now that the central illusion holding pain together has been seen through, you have new options that will become apparent as you explore this new place.

So—don't feel too upset. The standard assumptions about this may be wrong—but there is a great journey now in front of you with many amazing things to see.

Take some time.

Jamie: I'm back from visiting my niece, and I've had some time to reflect over the situation.

Thoughts are still telling me that this can't be it and that there's gotta be more. Why the fuck are people hell-bent on getting enlightened? Only because enlightenment is something they dream into existence. And when that dream bubble burst after 25 years, as in my case, there's just "WTF?" left. However:

If enlightenment is defined as seeing that the "I" doesn't exist as a separate entity, then I am enlightened. I wonder who came up with that word in first place—certainly not an enlightened person. "Annihilated" is more descriptive, don't you think? "Liberated" is OK, so is Jed McKenna's "truth-realised".

Still, those words had an air of splendour to me before. More dreaming. It's really so simple, there's nothing to it. I would feel like a conman if I were to hold satsangs about this and charge money for it. McKenna wrote three fucking BOOKS (four if you include the notebook) about the subject when three WORDS would suffice: I DON'T EXIST (let's make it four and add a DAMMIT!).

But I guess that book wouldn't become a bestseller—and I would probably be sued for plagiarism from hordes of direct pointers from Liberation Unleashed.

The search is over. But instead of being at the end of the road, at the goal, it's more like: this is where the journey starts for real, this is the beginning, not the end.

For the past 25 years I've been living a very restricted life, walked a very narrow line, because I wanted to obtain just this: enlightenment. Had I known before what enlightenment is I wouldn't have gone for it. I imprisoned myself for 25 years to obtain freedom now? How sick is that!?

I told you I was visiting my niece in another part of the country. She's a very bright and very sweet girl, 23'ish. Almost immediately I sensed that she had embarked on the self-development journey. She is borrowing books on the subject from the library (I'm glad she hasn't yet made her own spiritual library like I did!) and she is actively looking for hands-on courses in self-development. Well, WAS, because:

Elena, I couldn't see that sweet girl embarking on the same stupid journey I went on 25 years ago. Imprison herself and waste a lot of time and money. Sooner or later she would get to hear about enlightenment, and she would want it as much as I did, and only god knows for how many years she would be trapped, raped and robbed.

So when we reached the last few hours of my visit I gently told her "my dear, I sense that you are keen on self-development. Before you embark on that journey, please do me a favour and find out what 'I' is—well, we can do it right away, if you want, it won't take long", and she was all in.

We started by establishing what is real and what is unreal (the unicorn lesson), and she grabbed that immediately, including that some labels describe real things, other labels describe imaginary things. I then asked her to locate the "I" that is seemingly having all these experiences, and after a few minutes she said "I can't find anything".

When the implications of this discovery hit her she had a mild panic attack, mostly because, as she said: "Dammit, now everything has been destroyed!" and a few minutes later: "What a pity I paid that conman (a self-development coach) $60 for a consultation the other day, that money is just wasted!" (she's a student, and she is somewhat short of money).

No need to say that she has cancelled the self-development journey she'd booked a seat for, and now she has to sort out the implications, much like myself. I'll stay in touch with her, of course, to make sure she's alright—it was really a blow to her, and it came unexpectedly—but I'm glad she's not going to waste precious years of her valuable youth imprisoning herself for no reason.

So Elena, here we are. I send you much warmth for helping me out on this. Being an old geezer, I had expected this to last for months on end, if I had made it at all, and then all it took was a short look. The precise turning point was when I watched that movie and ate that cracker, and I saw/realised that there was watching and tasting but no seer and taster.

I don't know where life is going now, and it doesn't really matter. Old stuff is surfacing from the depths and structures are being reorganised. I will definitely not be holding satsangs, and I probably won't be writing books either (other than the one titled "I Don't Exist" with one single word inside: DAMMIT!).

I'm also not sure that I will recommend people to become 'enlightened' unsolicited, but it makes good sense to approach people who are about to imprison themselves in the self-development trap. We'll see where life goes…

Thanks again, Elena.

Eric

It was a real pleasure to work with Eric. He came to me very ready and he didn't even need a push. It was easy for me too. All became clear as we talked, and soon he said: "Yes, of course it's like this."

He came to me just to confirm what he already saw and only needed a little clarification. Lovely guy.—I. C.

Eric: Hi, Ilona, could you please guide me? I have looked and seen that there is no "me" running this body, no "me" thinking these thoughts, no real "me" found anywhere—and yet there is still this felt sense of a "me", something in charge and running the show, especially when there are difficult situations or when the body has severe health problems.

Then there seems to be a strong contraction—I am really tired of this whole thing and would like to resolve it once and for all. Would be grateful for some guidance. Thank you so much.

Ilona: Hi, Eric.

Thanks for your e-mail. Of course I can guide you, and we'll get this thing sorted once and for all. I will be asking some questions and you need to answer me with complete honesty.

The sense of "me" that you are talking about is the feeling of "I am" which has always been here and never changes, plus labelling by the mind. Could you look at thought itself with the thought and tell me what you see:

Are you in control of thoughts? Where do they come from? What is their function? What is behind thought?

Just answer me when you know answers with 100% certainty. No rush, have a good look and when you are ready—shoot.

Eric: Thanks, Ilona, for the quick reply. Here are my observations:

a) Definitely no control of thoughts.
b) They just arise out of nowhere.
c) Their function seems to be to enable this organism to navigate through this world but also to protect it.
d) If I look, I only find emptiness.

Ilona: Perfect.

Now look at the thought "I". It is also just a thought, a label that is not outside the flow of thoughts that are running freely and unstoppably. It's a label that is used in language to point to something. What is the thought "I" pointing to?

Eric: Well, to answer this honestly, I would have to say that it doesn't point to anything at all. After all, I'm not the body or the thoughts or the feelings or sensations, so to what can this "I" thought point? It is just another thought with no counterpart in reality. But seeing this doesn't seem to change anything...

Ilona: It's seeing it intellectually. You get that "I" does not point to anything, it's just a thought, yes. It has no power. Just a label.

Seeing this, allow the thought that there is no self at all in real life. Is it possible? Is this true?

What comes up?

Eric: Yes, Ilona, it is true!

But then, this is just another thought. This is crazy, seeing this or not is just a thought pattern, next to it life just goes on.

There cannot be a personal "me" in any of it, it is just not possible. I mean, Life just IS, and it is one movement, so how can there be a "me" standing apart from it?

Something is eluding me here, something still seems to be held here and doesn't want to be released, and it doesn't seem to be on a thought level. It's almost like I am waiting here for a release, a letting go, but then, how can something be released which is not there in the first place? No idea where to go from here. Something seems very close and obvious and yet...?

Thank you so much for all your help and time, really very grateful for this.

Ilona: Yes! Yes! You are right there!

No, there is no "me", just life flowing freely, including thoughts that label the experience. Has there ever been "me"?

There won't be any boom. The shift is subtle. It's not a big, shiny belief, it's just the recognition that reality is just like that. It's like if you believed that Santa was real as a child and then you found out he wasn't. Nothing really changed, only the illusion of Santa being real fell away. It's that kind of thing. And once it's seen, it cannot be unseen.

So what is Eric? Give me a full description, just state the obvious. Much love.

Eric: Yes, Ilona, thank you so much. Of course there is no "me", never was and never will be, just life moving in ever-changing patterns. Nothing really changes because it was always like that.

Just LIFE and certainly nobody living it or doing it. The remaining thing is that there is a strong felt sense of a presence (?) or being or whatever (do not want to use any spiritual platitudes), but undoubtedly there is this strong sense of something and it is always there and never ever changes.

But this is certainly not a personal presence or being, it is just there, vast and empty and yet also full of everything. Is there still a deception about something here? I do not think so... But anyway, thank you so much, Ilona, you cleared up a lot of things for me, it was so good to have you there as a kind of mirror and I feel a lot of respect, love, gratitude for the work you are doing. Thank you, thank you and much love to you.

Ilona: Eric, I'm delighted that seeing happened for you! We just need to go through a couple of bits before I let you go. The sense of something is "I am". It's the sense of being, it's unshakeable and yes, it is always here now. When you close your eyes it can be felt clearly. It's not going to go away.

Can you write answers to these questions now:

What is Eric? What is real? What is self?

Eric:

a) Eric is a character trait, learned, habitual thought and feeling patterns, genetic imprints, very much running on auto-pilot.
b) Real is what IS, before the overlay of concepts and labels.
c) Don't know exactly in what way you use the word 'self', if you mean a "personal self", then that would be only a thought. If you mean it in a broader sense, then that would be what I wrote before, this presence or what you called "I am".

Ilona: Just look deeper at the "self". Is there a self in real life at all?

You get it, right, that it's a word? That the very last thing the deep presence of reality is, or could possibly be, is you? What does the word 'self' point to? This mixing up of the self and the actual underlying reality of things is a common, and very unhelpful dogma. You can see clearer than what you wrote.

Eric: To what does the word "self" point to in real life? Well, to nothing really. If I speak to you about the tree in front of my window, you will know what I mean. The tree is just a label but it points to some real thing, like this body sitting here or the glass on the table or the pen next to the computer.

But "self"? No self can be found in real life, it just points to nothing real. It's just a word, but empty of any substance. There is this body, there is the thing called Eric with all its likes and dislikes, but there is just no self here which is in charge or doing all these things.

It just cannot be found once it is looked for and really examined. As you nicely wrote about Santa, as a child Santa seems real but once we grow up and really see that Santa is not real, we can never ever believe in Santa as real... that's about how it goes with the self; unexamined, it seems real but once really looked for, the seeing of the unreality of it is unavoidable.

Ilona: Congratulations and welcome to living free!

Thank you very much, it was a great popping.

Have you noticed any change in real life yet? And what was the last push you needed? Much love.

Eric: Thanks so much, Ilona. I don't know, there was not really any particular thing which pushed me over. It was more like a growing clarity happened during our conversation and then it was more like: "yes, of course it is like this", like a big YES.

Just more clarity now, more relaxed, more space, but I think it was already pretty thin and so there was not this big shift. Thanks again Ilona, what you are doing is incredible. If there were a "me" who believed in angels, I would say you are one.

Ilona: Thank you. I feel huge wave of appreciation here happening. Yes, you were right on the edge, made my work easy.

All the best to you, Eric. If you ever want to chat, do not hesitate. Always ready to help if needed.

Eric: Thanks my friend, this is great. And all the best to you too. Well, much more than all the best.

Michael

Michael is a serious meditation practitioner, deeply imbedded in Zen, (Tibetan and Vipassana traditions), all together about 40 years. Working together, we took three days to penetrate his illusion of self. It is intense. Be aware. But on the bright side, many people have reported to me that it helped them to see the truth.—E. N.

Michael: Hello, Elena.

I have been reading your work. I deeply resonate with your comments, responses and experience.

I am a long-time meditator in Zen/Tibetan/Vipassana traditions. Like you, I have done numerous retreats over the past decades. In the process, there has been a grounding and opening in my life. There have been times of sudden deep insights, i.e. kensho, lasting for weeks.

There have been times of the "I" dissolving and "just being". But, alas, there is always a return to the old "me as the centre" dance again and again, retreat after retreat. Looking at your work, I am drawn to the many statements of achievement and breakthrough by meditators who are fairly new at it.

Conversely, I experience inadequacy at my many years without approaching such goals. Meanwhile, I am feeling a bit like I'm going in circles and feeling a bit worn out in the mental dharma game. I am scheduled for a six-week Vipassana retreat in September, but I am hesitant to continue on the wheel of illusion, i.e. getting it at the retreat and losing it soon after.

Then your comments touched a chord. Yes, I can glimpse the truth of no "I". There is just seeing, hearing and touching, without a seer, hearer or toucher. But it is largely intellectual. I turn toward it and seem to get it for seconds, then it fades, dissolves, morphs into reflection, analysis... I have a sense that if I could dialogue with you via e-mail, Skype or the phone, it would be very helpful in this process. Seems to be an edge here, as there always is, to step over.

I have been pouring over your site and the other blogs cited. There is truth to be tasted... can we chat?

With gratitude, Michael

Elena: Hey, Michael, yes, let's chat.

This goes as following: you try not to read web forums or work with other teachers while you work with me. We do this together, a clear channel between us.

I will ask you some questions, and you will give me the truest answer you can find. It can take no time, some time or a somewhat longer time, it doesn't matter—as long as you stick it out to the end, and give it your best shot.

Tell me what your search is about. What you are searching for, really?

Michael : Hi, Elena. Thanks for being open to this exchange.

I will speak from my truest (in my awareness) place without editing.

The seeking is to find a lasting place without suffering. There is a thirst for a space where there just is what is without the storylines, hopes, fears, pushes, pulls and numbings that take me away from the present.

The seeking is about the desire to stay put in this moment; to deeply, fully and continuously be with the sense of eternal now. The seeking is about seeing through memories and future goals as dreams. The seeking is about living fully in this body, this breath, this humanness. The seeking is about dissolving the belief that I/Michael is the centre of the universe.

The seeking is about dropping the damn seeking, cutting away and free from the seeming magnetic pull that THIS is not enough and that I need to do another retreat, deepen concentration, be more present, cut away the hindrances yada yada. The seeking is about collapsing the act of seeking something other than what is.

Intellectually, there's such an accumulation of stuff/beliefs/understandings—suffocating—the deepest pull is to just rest here in the ordinariness of typing this e-mail and noticing the subtle, high-pitched sound in my ears. The seeking sometimes feels like being the best, a good boy, a dynamite dharma student—psychodynamic shit.

As I am typing, there is noticing the felt sense of "seeking". Noticing that my belly a bit tight, seems like I am leaning, forward-reaching or trying to get. It seems effortful. How to relax the effort? Who efforts? Is it just the thoughts called I/me/mine? That simple.

There is confusion about the seeking now. Really, not sure what is being sought, who is seeking and what's the point anyway. Exhausting. Just want to be...

There it is from the moment... appreciate your energy and time with this, Michael

Elena: "The seeking sometimes feels like being the best, a good boy, a dynamite dharma student—psychodynamic shit."

I've been here—believe me. You just described exactly where I was a while back, so take some solace that we're on the same page.

As you look and see through the illusion, the seeking WILL drop, and the effort WILL drop. Relaxation will happen naturally. And the relaxation I am talking about is not the peace on the surface of the mind.

I too felt suffocated by the never-ending seeking. I thought it would never stop. I thought it was a part of the life of a human being, all seeking. Seeking is unresolved energy—when it resolves itself, when consciousness sees what it was hiding from itself, the seeking will be no more.

Michael: You say "seeking is unresolved energy—when it resolves itself, when consciousness sees what it was hiding from itself, the seeking will be no more." So then how to access the "resolution"? Seems like this is where seeing "I" as just thought comes in, is that right? So is it just about the practice of seeing the "I" as thought every time it comes up?

Over the last couple days, I have more or less (when I remember) noted the sense of "I" and labelled it "thinking/thought" a la Vipassana. There is a real lightening up that comes with this. Seems like my self-referenced story lines have diminished in frequency and intensity.

Practising looking AT the "I", looking at any sensation—again akin to Vipassana noting. Is the concept of "practice" relevant or just more getting in the way? Seems like there needs to be something systematic—akin to meditation—or is it just sudden "getting it" when conditions are ripe?

I am sitting with your comment about consciousness seeing what it is hiding from itself. Seems like consciousness hides nothing; or is there more to it? Seems like thought is just content or passing appearance of mind, not real or solid any more than we make it so. Consciousness just is, right?

It seems to take very deep relaxation to drop seeking. What comes first, the relaxation or the dropping of seeking?

Elena: The resolution is exactly what we are doing here.

Once it's seen, it's never unseen. You only step through the gate once.

Vipassana is a good aid, yes. You can break down the experience, and see what is there. But at the same time, you should turn your laser Vipassana attention back to what is actually looking and doing it. Is there any doer?

Does thinking require a thinker or is it just thinking? Does feeling require a feeler or is it just feeling happening? Is anybody required for treeing the tree or is it just treeing?

It rains. Does it require a doer to rain?

Look. Check.

Do not disperse the energy of looking into double-guessing. Trust in what is already happening. It is already happening. You just need to focus.

Consciousness just is. And what is happening now is. Life is living itself... all is. All real. The only thing that is not is you. You are not part of reality. Look.

Relaxation is the dropping of seeking, freeing tons of energy for just being.

Michael: No doer, no thinker, no imaginer, no planner, no rememberer, no typer, no dialoguer, no man , no woman, no age, no race, no taste, no touch, no hearer, no fearer, no lover... just coming back to this and coming back and coming back when I am present; and I am present when I recognise the non-actor.

You say "do not flounder around... do not get into double-guessing." If that's the case, there doesn't seem to be much to say.

So I just keep making this the main event, so to speak, in my "living". 24/7, no letup, just burn it up... yes? You know it doesn't grab me in a "passionate" way to do this; it's quieter and softer and hardly noticeable.

So I have a question for you. I understand this is a digression from our core focus of dissolving the "sense of 'I' as doer". You do not need to answer yes or no, but your input would be appreciated. I ask you this with your background in Vipassana.

I am wavering about following through with a six-week Vipassana retreat at Barre, Massachusetts, in September. My original inspiration is suspect. I intended to do it to work on progressing on the Jhanic Arc of insight development.

In part, I was coming from a place of impatience with my "lack of progress". Reading your website left me wondering "heck, why are all these young folks , new to the practice, reporting amazing realisations while Michael, after about forty—that's right—years of regular practice and retreats feels like he's at square one?"

Anyway, I am "grooving" with this very new experiment of dropping the seeker/seeking. Hence why do a retreat if it's just more seeking? On the other hand, might the retreat be used to deepen and expand the process I am doing with your support? Any input?

Meanwhile, back to LOOKING AT I, here, there, wherever it pops up and out... right here, Michael.

Elena: You're dealing with this as a belief. Trying to get the right belief, get the belief strong enough that it saves you. But there's no you to save—AND—belief, even if true, is just belief. Recognition, seeing—they hit at a very different level, and it's that level alone where freedom lies.

After forty years of hitting this? Of course you'll feel disheartened. Initially there is a burning for truth, then we lose the confidence that we can actually make it, especially after hearing "the path is LOOOOOOONG, it takes lifetimes" and so on all the time. This idea that the path to freedom takes lifetimes—it is a lie. The path is one step long, just one. And that one step is the seeing of the reality that there is no you.

Long term seekers, like I was and you are, seek habitually, we've already built a whole structure around it, and we fall into this low-grade, never-satisfied dharma path to do something with the self, to get rid of it, to make it more deeper or whatever words we can come up with.

And then some young folks come up, and we don't believe them, we hate them, we protect our forty years of seeking. We feel it's not fair. But whatever we feel, something fresh is already there and starts to bother us into looking at our seeking again.

You want to go to a retreat for 6 weeks? You can end this in ten seconds. That said—it's good that you're beginning to question the value of 'satori chasing'; that's a big trap. I love that you're building a fresh outlook on it.

"I intended to do it to work on progressing on the Jhanic Arc of insight development."

And the "Jhanic Arc of insight development" sounds a little like a marketing slogan.

Square one is the best place to be, Michael. It's where all the action starts.

And besides, life is living itself in different ways. For some reason, this embodiment of yours was involved in this particular movement of life—forty years' dharma-seeking. Somebody else was forty years' carrier-seeking, somebody else was forty years' seeking in a different way.

Seeking is inevitable until consciousness sees itself for what it is. For that moment to happen, some embodiments need forty years in

Vipassana, some need five minutes of direct seeing. There is nothing about you, because there is no "you".

Let's go into some of the things you said.

"...when I am present; and I am present when I recognise the non-actor."

You are not present. There is no "you". There's just the present.

You do not recognise the non-actor. There's no you to recognise it. There's no you at all.

Presence is. Recognition is.

Do not believe anything I say; check. Look deeper.

Michael: When I look, it is... so looking is happening more... such a free space... seems daring and risky and nothing special all at same time... looking at my fingers on the keyboard. Looking at thought—the same thing.

Elena: It's like the release of a burden. It is that simple. They call it "the cosmic joke" for a reason.

Now, staring at your fingers waiting for the 'you' to get it isn't going to work, for a reason I think you can guess. Instead, investigate. Is there a "you" in any shape or form in reality? Is there an owner of the experience?

Tell me.

Michael: Got it! Just listening to an Eckhart Tolle CD speaking about presence. Akin to what we are nudging toward... More and more just looking, hearing... letting the train roll on...

Elena: Michael. I told you. If you want to work with me, I need a clear channel to you. If you're spamming your mind with the work of different spiritual teachers, you will not have the clarity to see the truth.

Remember, this pointing is not meant to zap you into the state. It has to be clear realisation, actual seeing of actual reality. I need you to work; focus on one thing and one thing only.

Can you find "you" in any shape or form in reality? And if yes, we need to continue to work. So tell me.

Michael: Yes, thanks, Elena. My head is doing its thing while the attention band notices. There is more time with attention as just attention. Thoughts come, attention notices, thoughts go. I continue to swing between the ease and grace of just perception and getting caught in storylines (minutes ago, got caught up in some stock investing obsessing... then saw it , then released).

I do not sense being "through the gate"... I do notice the trying (I identification), then release it and just see...

Clearly greater equanimity, but the stateless state is not in my felt sense except for flashes, sometimes longer. But there is still coming and going.

In grocery store today, watched the shoppers shopping and they seemed different somehow. There was a sense of every person doing what they had to do, sort of everyone enlightened. They were just doing. I, too, was just doing. Simple ordinary, easy, just what is happening, no fuss.

So yes, thoughts are doing their thing, but I am more detached, i.e. see them as just passing stuff. Bring my attention back to the immediate, sensory flow...

How is this different from the idea of "anatta"? Do not want to do theory, just wondering.

This place is like how it is after a retreat. Spacious, immediate, balanced.

There is a background wanting of this to stick, stay, be permanent. Then judgement for this. Then letting it go and more looking AT what is…

So it is a clear realisation. Then it morphs. Then back. Riding the waves. Deep breathing, in the body, going nowhere, doing nothing...

Got into letting the driving drive me today on the way to shopping. Fun...

Elena: "Yes, thanks, Elena. My head is doing its thing".

The head is not yours. There is no "you". Stop reaching for a state.

"I do not sense being 'through the gate'..."

No, you don't. You're not. You keep trying to 'fake it' until it 'catches'. This is not how it happens, and until you open yourself to doing this in a different way, you'll never see it. You've been ploughing this furrow for

40 years, Michael. You're not going to get free by doing the same thing you've done for 40 years, but harder.

I'm not asking you to release the 'I' identification, as you put it. You're putting words in my mouth, interpreting what I say in terms of what you've been doing all along, but what you've been doing all along is not going to free you. You have to snap out of this, Michael, and work this from a radically different angle. I mean, look—you say this:

"Clearly greater equanimity, but the stateless state is not in my felt sense except for flashes, sometimes longer. But there is still coming and going."

This has nothing to do with liberation. It's like you're having a conversation with yourself, and not listening to what I'm saying. I never asked you to enter a stateless state—I never asked you anything like that.

It's like you don't want to listen.

You have to decide, Michael. Are you interested in doing this differently, because if you're not, and you're happy with another 20 years of fruitless seeking, and then death, then let's have that out now, so we can both get on with doing what we need to do.

This new angle is best described as follows. You say this:

"So yes, thoughts are doing their thing, but I am more detached, i.e. see them as just passing stuff."

I say this—How can "you" be detached or not detached? There actually is no "you", seriously. Check it. Actually check if this is true.

"Bring my attention back to the immediate, sensory flow..."

"MY" attention? Michael. Attention just is. It's not yours. Look.

Being at the Gate is not feeling "spacious, immediate, balanced". The many mystical pictures and paintings and poems that you've read and made, they are locking you in a prison of fiction. You have to snap out of that, you have to really snap out of it.

So tell me what the self is. You should be able to talk and explain as if you are talking and explaining to a ten-year old girl with no understanding of any spiritual tradition. Drop the vocabulary, the conventions. Be original, talk about things in your own words.

You are talking in the habitual "spiritual" language, and it's all just part of your cage. It makes it incredibly complex—but looking and truth are simpler than what you're doing.

"So it is a clear realisation."

Realisation of what? Answer my questions. You can't recognise something you're not prepared to look at.

"Then it morphs. Then back. Riding the waves. Deep breathing, in the body, going nowhere, doing nothing..."

Are you writing poetry? Stop writing poetry. It won't help you. I need you to work. Step through the Gate.

"Got into letting the driving drive me today on the way to shopping. Fun..."

Drive WHO today? Drive WHO, MICHAEL?

How does driving drive something that does not exist?

FIND OUT. INVESTIGATE.

Michael: Hi. Frustrated... am I just going in circles here? What am I missing? Feels like semantics; the words "I", "Me" and "Mine" give away the game.

In fact, I am doing my best to listen...

This is bringing up a sense of inadequacy in this realm.

Let me work with this some more, and let go some more. Feeling like a bad student with the wrong answer. This place is not useful to me... need to regroup.

OK. There is a getting of the simplicity of just being without referencing "I". Excuse my poetry and tendency to wax profound... just patterns.

The realisation of everything is as it is, not good or bad... just what is. The body called "me" is just what it is. "Me" is a tired self-reference being worn down.

No, there is no "reaching for a state" intentionally, but habits continue.

You say "step to the gate"; "I need you to work"... I am with you, Elena, but experiencing anger and frustration at not being quick, sharp or good enough to get your validation. Need to let this go. And at the same time, this is grist for the mill, as my reaction is merely a reflection of "I"...

Just typing, noticing the dark background, the bright computer screen, hearing the computer tapping, noticing my chest rise and fall...

OK... I get it... after re-reading your comments, how can I be anything? Virtually anything attributed to me is attributed to nobody, an illusion, so I am left with just the experience occurring here and now. There is just the river of unfolding moments to be witnessed by no one. Too obvious. Staying with what is in front now here, in front now here, in front now here is all. I will take this to bed tonight... Good night!

No, I will not take this to bed... it will be taken to bed.

Elena: "In fact, I am doing my best to listen..."

This endeavour is not about listening... and then going and continuing to do what you were doing before! You have to hit this from a different angle, and that angle is 'what is real?' What is really going on? Is it actually true that there's really no me?

This is how it goes: I will ask you a question. Then you will go and look and answer with absolute honesty, OK?

Inadequacy is just a feeling arising. You can look into it and ask where it comes from. WHO is feeling inadequate? WHO? There is no "you" to feel inadequacy; it's just a feeling arising to give you some information. Ask what.

Then ask who is feeling that way. And don't just ask, and sit there waiting for the answer to land. Go get the answer. Find out.

You say you want to let go some more? I say this—letting go of what? Answer me: of what?

The simplicity of being arises out of knowing there is no "I". So find out, make certain.

Be clear, precise and honest. Use language as if you were talking to somebody who had never ever heard of meditation, retreats, non-duality or any other spiritual stuff—fifteen years old or twelve years old.

You feel frustrated? Good, good. Look at the feeling. Is there a *you* feeling it? Are you doing the feeling? Or is feeling arising? Can you stop the feeling? Can you stop the thought in the middle?

Find out.

Just drop all the assumptions. I am not judging you in any way here. This work is not linear like Vipassana. There's just one step, and that's finding out the truth of this. Trust the flow. Any feeling or thought that comes up is here to show you something.

Look.

You ARE making progress, don't be disheartened. When you say—

"Just typing, noticing the dark background, the bright computer screen, hearing the computer tapping, noticing my chest rise and fall...

OK... I get it... after re-reading your comments, how can I be anything? Virtually anything attributed to me is attributed to nobody, an illusion, so I am left with just the experience occurring here and now. There is just the river of unfolding moments to be witnessed by no one. Too obvious. Staying with what is in front now here, in front now here, in front now here is all. I will take this to bed tonight... Good night! J"

This was good, Michael. This is right on the money.

So what is "I"?

Can you find it in any shape or form in reality?

Michael: Good morning, friend. Where is the "I"? ... Hello? Seems to be lost, gone, absent, missing... When there is looking at it, there is nothing, just this. It's like falling backward, just falling. Seems different, a bit weird or unusual, but just for a moment.

Then back to this computer, these fingers, that bird chirping. Then a blip of memory. All these come and go like a river of stuff passing by. There is no pull or push at this moment.

Just here now.

Sip of coffee.

Thought of something to do later... sound of bird chirp.

Is this intellectual? How to know...seems actually present...

Thoughts are fewer.

Where is the "I"? Where is it? What is it? Just a big hole, a sense of dropping, like falling down a canyon... then gone, then back...

And on and on... such a miniscule shift, barely noticeable. Just did some sitting meditation; it was easy. Seems like a somewhat different landscape. Tricky to describe. More immediacy, less pulled away... a bit more vividness and directness.

Nothing is different, yet it is somehow transformed. It's more "here". That keeps coming: more here, more here, even just here. With passing thoughts of this or that, past or future... less of a buying into or being pulled.

A familiar land, yet strange... continuing to self on and off without buying into it...

Our exchange yesterday evening touched something... felt my frustration and watched it collapse with no one to latch onto... poof!

Still so new and fresh. Watching thoughts of doubt and disbelief...then back to here... yes, no boom boom, fireworks… more like a steady flow streaming over and around the rocks...whoops, poetic.

Elena: Let's make sure. Tell me more here.

If you look, can you find "you" in reality without referencing thought, feeling or sensation? Go ahead and tell me now. Without avoiding writing "I" or "me", write where "you" is in reality.

Michael: Where is the "I" in reality? Not under the chair, not behind the curtain, not on my lap. Where is the "I"? Where is the "I"? Nice mantra.

A phantom in the night. A shape shifter. A ghost. A whirlwind. Cannot find a damn thing to hold onto or point to. There are thoughts relating to self, but a quick search with attention comes up blank. An empty bucket full of the comings and goings of ideas.

I wonder if this will fade. Somehow I want to put it to the test... haha... trying won't make it appear or disappear, so I hang on with this. "I" is missing in action, i.e. more like seen through as smoke. Ahhh, the air is fresh here. It is a quiet shift. Nothing shifted... just seeing what is not there.

When I experienced some intense emotion/upset over some stuff several hours ago, I just was with it. There was a quick sense of "uh oh, I will re-attach to 'I'". No, just impermanent emotion comings and going like wind through a window.

Lighter, brighter, and still the personality does its thing. But no "I" in the personality. Just patterns, beliefs and habits doing their thing. No big deal. None of it is me when there is no me.

Where am I, where am I, where am I... not here or there or then or anywhere... ahh.

Elena: Again. Deeper. Self is a thought. Is this true? Look again.

If this is real there's no need to hold on to it. You don't have to grip something that IS for it still to be.

If you go to see a movie, do you think it's real? No, you know it's a movie, an illusion. You may have moments of identification, but they are just moments. Overall, you understand you are in a theatre, and that what's going on is an illusion. If you'd never been outside the movie theatre, then you would view what was going on as real. But not if you ever stepped outside and the mind noticed the difference.

You've stepped outside the movie theatre, but your mind still has the story of you in it. The story doesn't go just because it's fiction. But because it's seen to be fiction, its ability to trap is fatally weakened.

So stay on it, get real with it, hit it, dig into it—if it's real it can take it. It's just seeing WHAT IS NOT THERE.

Any time you have an emotion or a feeling, look behind it. What is there? Exactly—nothing.

Uniqueness of the embodiment of life is real. But self? Something owning life? A central control, a manager?—no. And don't take my word for it—don't fall into that trap. Instead, investigate.

Is this true?

You are getting somewhere, I'm very happy with how you're moving now. Let's stay on it, and make sure you're really through, really seeing the truth of this.

Michael: Good morning. All quiet here. Just a gap where self-reference was. It's a gap, a hole, an opening. So there is more attention to just sensory stuff: seeing, hearing, moving. Quite simple, really.

You say self is a thought. Yes. An idea that gets reinforced by not seeing it, by just reacting. Who reacts?

Checked out your blog. Bravo for spreading the news! Great work and great work with me, your persistence and directness helped to keep me looking. Seems like looking is the key. Looking at self/the "I" thought and seeing it for what it is not. Initially, it was frustrating because I couldn't hold the focus. Now, fairly easy. Again, no big deal. Life is much more peaceful, non-reactive.

Your movie theatre analogy is good. Get to see life living rather than Me doing. Although this is not a 24/7 awareness. There are spots where the "I" solidifies, but it seems to dissolve pretty quickly. When you are not caught up in the storyline with Me as the main actor/star/hero/villain, it's easy to enjoy the show.

I reflect on choice... with no "I", I have no choice. Just happenings through this mind/body/social sensory blob of causes and conditions.

Elena: Oh, Michael, I am so happy for you. This is the beginning, but without this beginning, you know, there'd just be endless perfecting of the self, endless purifying, which is the cruellest of dead ends.

You did it. So to speak. Nice work, Michael. I'm very happy. Welcome to the flow.

João

João came prepared; he jumped straight in and finished it in no time. His key problem was that he was looking for the big hit, for the lights from on high. The reality of the absence of self, and the unbroken flow of being—although it sounds very grandiose—is actually quite pedestrian and normal in and of itself. Once I gave him just a little lead on it, he saw it almost immediately. We also talked about free will and he went off to enjoy his life after having seen through the separation.—I. C.

João: Hey. My brother told me about you guys and I came across your blog. I read some of your posts to find out how the process of liberation takes place.

This concept of "there's no self" is easy for me to understand, but only intellectually (am I making myself clear?). When I look further into this concept during normal day-to-day activities, putting 'myself' in a state of awareness almost like an observer, I really start to wonder who is controlling this body and where all these thoughts come from. Yet I still find identification with the self.

OK, this is "me" thinking that I need your guidance. I hope you can help me.

Thanks for your time, blessings.

Ilona: Hi, João. Thank you for writing to me. Yes, we can work together to resolve this thing. Let's get you free once and for all.

I will be asking you questions and I need you to answer with perfect honesty, and only when you've had a good look. That means when you get a clear answer that you think is 100% true.

Let's start with examining thoughts. Can you control thoughts? Where do they come from? Can you see that thoughts are labels? Can you make the labelling stop?

Please reply when you're ready.

João: I think I've got it.

Ilona: What is João? What is real? What is self?

Just answer when you are ready.

João: It's kind of hard for me to put it into words.

João is a character experiencing itself. Everything is real, this body is real, these thoughts are real, only the idea that there's a "me" creating all this is an illusion. Self is a label that points to an assumption that there is really a "me". But this "me" is just a belief given by society.

It's something we can't even question because we've never had the opportunity to realise that self is just a thought about this mind, this body, these thoughts.

This is the best I can describe it.

Ilona: Wow. Beautiful!

You are getting it. Please rant about it, how you see what's happening on this planet, what you see when you look at your family, just expand a lot, it helps to clarify stuff in your head.

Carry on, please.

João: Nothing's really changed. The world is seen by João with a totally new perspective now. Everything seems possible since there's no self to be affected. João feels that everything is right in this very moment, yet thoughts arise in "my" head that there's something more to achieve; that this experience is leading 'me' to somewhere.

But since that "me" is just a label, "I" understand that there's nothing more to do. João feels something external that is affecting his understanding in some way.

What can I tell you about my family? I love them, nothing's changed about the way "I" feel about them. "I" understand that "my" parents did the best they could with the knowledge they had to teach "me" about life.

Ilona: Please clarify that.

João: "I" ran some tests on João's mind. "I" posed questions to "myself" that destroy the possibility of the existence of a self. Then "I" started to see it. I was not controlling anything.

It wasn't me that was walking, it wasn't me that was moving my arms. "I" was just watching, just like in a movie. But I still have doubts. OMG there is always a feeling of a "me" watching everything, but "I" know that's impossible.

I really can't express myself. Got frustrated.

Ilona: Yeah, this feeling of frustration is a distraction from noticing the obvious. Fear is trying to protect the idea of the existence of a self, like 'if I drop this belief I'll lose control of everything'. Behind fear, life happens, everything happens, without the need of a "me" to control events.

Fear is just a protection mechanism—but it's not about 'beating fear'—it's seeing that nothing needs to be protected. It's nothing.

Everything is happening without a manager. The fear of losing control of life is just that—fear. Just a feeling plus labelling by the mind. And thoughts come and go by themselves, right?

Check now if there is a watcher here. Does life need a watcher at all? Or is it a feeling of watching plus labelling? What do you find?

João: Yes, thoughts come and go by themselves, there's only the illusion that there is a "me" with free will. The idea of self is sustained by a chain of thoughts that always ends up with a "me".

No, there's no watcher, watching just happens. Life doesn't need any watcher at all, everything happens by itself.

Ilona: Great!

No, there is no watcher and no need for it either. Let's see what you notice about free will, choice and decisions. How does it all work?

João: There's no free will, because there's no one with a will. There are also no choices and decisions to be made. Everything just happens by itself. The illusion of self makes the events of life look like decisions. But there's no one to make decisions!

Ilona: It sounds to me like you are through. How does it feel? Are you done? Is there any doubt at all? Do you notice anything different? What was the last push?

João: "I" am not really sure if "I" am done because actually "I" was waiting for a major change. But "I" can see now that it's just the dropping of an old belief. There's nothing different, actually, everything stays the same, but now everything is seen from a new perspective. "I" feel way more relaxed and way more present in the moment. I am not sure about the last push, I think it happened when I recognised fear and frustration as a mechanism of protection.

I would just like to ask you some questions.

I know there is no one to make decisions, yet there's a feeling that we do. So how do we not decide? For example, if I have to choose between right and left, how can I not choose to make the best choice for me? Am I making myself clear?

You still want right, even though you're through. How do you deal with it?

Ilona: All decisions happen effortlessly. The brain makes choices. After the decision is made, labelling kicks in and the mind starts discussing what is right and what it should be. It will gradually fall away.

Once the decision is made, the heart knows. Then you just need to recognise what feels right and go with it. It all becomes natural after a while. The more conditioning falls away, the more everything feels effortless. So after the core belief in separation falls, there is a cleaning-up period. It unfolds by itself. It's a ride without rider!

It is not you choosing for you, but life living life. Did that answer your question?

João: Oh, yeah, you did.

I have to really thank you for the time you've spent helping me Ilona. Thanks to you, this journey looks a lot more fun.

You are doing a great job liberating all these people.

Ilona: Thank you João! Thank you for looking. My heart fills with appreciation.

I'm happy to assist, and any time you have a burning question, just ask.

Charles

Charles is a long-time Vipassana meditation practitioner. In the middle of our work, exhausted, he came up with such profound honesty that I will never forget it. It was an amazing moment. I bet many of us could sign our names under the list he came up with when I asked him why he seeks enlightenment. Fantastic liberation.—E. N.

Charles: Hello.

I have done a few of the same Vipassana Goenka retreats as you. That's why I thought it might be better to get in touch with you, as you would understand better where I am.

My problem is that I have been working with this no-self/non-duality (Advaita) for quite some time now. When I look consciously for self, I don't see any self. Intellectually, I have accepted that there is no self or any entity sitting inside my head experiencing this world.

As a brief sampler, this is what I wrote in my diary yesterday.

"What am I, or what does it really mean when I say 'I'? I am a human being (living organism). I have this human body which has, besides other organs, a brain. The brain is a thinking machine. I don't know most of the stuff about how it functions, but that's OK. I drive a car without knowing how it works and will travel by air without knowing how the planes work.

This brain seems to have some kind of systems made up with all kinds of logic hardwired, firmware and loads of software... (DNA, culture, religion, upbringing, habits, nature, education, friends and what have you)."

I do not know, even after this knowledge/realisation I don't feel liberated or realised. where do I go from here?

Elena: Hi, Charles. Let's chat. While we chat, try not to read about these things. Your source on this stuff, for the duration of our conversation, is your own honest investigations into what's going on inside, and not anything in a book or on a website, no matter how profound.

Ok? This works much better if you really look and come up with the truest answer you can find for yourself.

The first and most important thing is this—do not believe me, no matter how much you want to, and do not agree because something sounds like it should be true.

Instead, check everything I say, OK?

You wrote: "I am a human being (living organism)." No, this is not true. There is a body, a mind—all that stuff, but nothing 'owns' that. There's no central control, no self that drives it. All the processes just flow between themselves of their own accord. Simply put, there is no "you". Investigate this.

What do you feel if I say there is no "you"? What comes up?

Charles: There is a buzzing sensation in the brain as I read what you have written. I agree that there is no "me" who owns/drives or commands this body. There is no "me" who does the thinking. The thinking happens.

But I am not able to get out of this sense of self. E.g., when you say driving happens, if I agree, it would be more of an intellectual agreement.

No direct seeing/realisation there. I continue to feel that I am driving the car.

I will keep re-reading this e-mail a few more times, focusing on it; will get back to you after that.

Elena: Good. Do not believe me. Check everything.

Look at anything in front of you and around you—anything that you can say for sure is a part of reality—it exists. For example, your computer or a cup or a rug. It exists. You don't need to try hard to see it. In fact, even if you close your eyes, it's there anyway.

Now compare the following:

Take Spiderman. If you think about him, you have thoughts, feelings. They're real, right? Real thoughts, feeling, real image of a red and blue lycra suit. But Spiderman is not real. Spiderman does not exist. He is not part of reality. The thoughts and images are—but he isn't.

Self is exactly the same as this. Exactly the same. What arise are thoughts, feelings and sensations in the body. They are real thoughts and feelings. But an actual self? That's not real. Self does not exist. You are not part of reality. The thoughts and images about you are—but a being that is living life? Thinking thoughts? No. There's nothing there.

Do not believe this. Look.

Charles: I understand all that you say. I really do not believe in self. In fact, I believe there is no self, because whenever I have tried to see it, I haven't found this self/entity. Now, when I look, I cannot see any self here. (For me, to look means to focus; apply my mind to the question.)

But it is also true that I behave and do things as if the self were there, so this sense of self is not over inside me. It is not dead/gone; it is still there, but when I focus my attention on this thing (i.e. look), it's not there. But when I am not thinking about this, self happens as a habit. I know it sounds very confusing, but I am being honest.

Elena: This is all just belief. You're trying to believe your way there. Won't work. No belief is permanent. Seeing alone is permanent. But you can use belief to get a fix on this—just ask "where does the belief come from?"

Charles: Many times' past experience on this subject causes me to arrive at the same conclusion about there being no controlling entity, no doer, no observer, no little man in the head, nothing of that sort. This repeated experience creates this belief.

Elena: So if you look and can't find you:

What is typing? What is believing? What is thinking?

Be as precise as possible.

Charles: Even after looking very hard for it, there is no I/Me to be found. Then what is typing/thinking/believing or driving… I am really stuck here. In my day-to-day life, I behave as if I am doing all these and other activities, like getting angry or happy or feeling other emotions.

Work, travel, everything that I do has a sense of feeler/doer behind it. But when I look, there is no feeler, there is no doer, no 'self' entity. Both things can't be true, but that is my current experience. I don't know how to proceed from here.

Elena: Let's look further.

"Both things can't be true".

Yes, you are right. They can't.

"I don't know how to proceed."

You need to find out which one is true, and which one isn't.

As in—you need to actually find out. Not just pick the one you think is the more profound belief and convince yourself of it. Actually find out, in reality, which one is true. Another good way to do this is to see what IS there. So if there's no self, where is all this stuff coming from? Where is it going?

When you drive the car or type or walk, look for what is there.

Take the time. Find out. Is this really what is happening? Please respond to me when you've taken the time to look into both instances—when you can't find a self, and when you think that self is operating. Find out what is there, present, existing, besides the self.

Charles: There is my body, the keyboard, the water bottle, the computer, the screen, thoughts about typing, the action of typing, sound coming from the window, birds, road traffic, looking at stuff to be done, more thoughts, thinking…

Basically, there are two types of thought. One seems to be arising on its own, and another seems to be done or guided purposefully (as in thinking about work or making decisions). Lots of stuff, but no self or separate entity. Typing now, the body is here, the keyboard and the screen are here, the action of typing is taking place, and thoughts and more thoughts…

Elena: Good. Now look for the "sense of self". What is it? A thought, maybe a bodily sensation or feeling—look for it and break it down, divide and dissect what it really is.

Charles: This sense of self is at its strongest when the thought is about needs and desires. For example, when thinking about work and money or lack of it, this "sense of I" is at its strongest.

What is that wants to strive to make money? Isn't it "I have to make more money"? The need for working and earning is real, but somehow this very sense of "I" is getting strongly associated/embedded with the basic need to earn a livelihood. Then come fear and anxiety about not being able to do it.

This subsequent cascade of thoughts reinforces the sense of "I". These thoughts do not help solve the problem; in fact they hurt my chances. They are just hindrances.

A realisation: the thoughts and emotions that built up this sense of "I" are hurting the chance of success at work. Work will go much better if "I" gets out of the way. While doing this process, a strong buzzing is felt inside the head; also experiencing mild vibrations on the crown of the head. It may be better for me to now just focus on "this sense of I" and watch for it, how and where all it keeps coming up. I will try and continue to do so.

Elena: Please stop trying to analyse your way free. It doesn't make sense, and it doesn't work. You need to look and you will see.

The only thing that matters is seeing things as they are, not the story around them. When you looked, what you saw was thoughts. Then you went into your intellectual faculties and thoughts started to coagulate into stories. Intellect has nothing to do with LOOKING.

Just make sure we are looking here.

And what you saw were thoughts, sensations, feelings, right?

Thoughts do exist. Sensations do exist. Feelings do exist. You don't.

Look.

You are not part of reality.

Thoughts, sensations and feelings are part of reality. You are not.

Charles: Yes, I can say from my experience "there is no breather, breathing is just happening", but I honestly cannot say that about driving. I understand what we are getting at here, but in my default mode of living today, it does not feel like driving happens on its own. There is a sense of doing. In this context, I would like you to clarify for me: what exactly do we mean by seeing?

Does this seeing involve thinking about it or some felt sense or something?

Elena: What is the sense of doing?

Look at it. What is it? Dissect it. What is the sense of "I", the sense of doing? This sense that makes you feel that there is a "you" who lives, who drives and so on.

Look at what it really is. Keep looking at it.

What if it's just a thought?

Explore it.

Charles: I am exhausted and frustrated about not getting this; I am just not getting it. I know I made some progress and cleared something up, but I just desperately want to get it done with. I really don't know—what do I do? If it was about climbing twenty mountains, I would gladly do that. Anyway, I plan to keep at it.

Yes, this sense of being is made up of thoughts and feelings (body sensations). Moreover, it seems to be a strong habit of living, doing things from a standpoint which assumes this "I" being the truth. This "I" is nowhere to be seen. Now, how to see clearly something that is not there in the first place, how to make it my permanent state of being?

Elena: This is very good. Intensity is good. The fact that you're frustrated is great. It's not you being frustrated. There is no "you". It's just frustration—dissonance between the old belief structure and the truth.

And—there is no "you" to make progress. There is no you at all. Look.

And listen—it's not about climbing 20 mountains. It's about taking one step, just once. The seeing that the you is a fiction.

This idea that it's so hard, that it needs lifetimes to climb is so appealing to people. And they climb. But who is climbing? The self itself, making itself more "special", "more spiritual", "more hardcore".

We will make it, no worries.

In Vipassana it's all very simple, very logical and very linear—like all the instructions before every sit, exactly what to do. It's not going to work like this. Don't look at me as an instructor with set of instructions. This is a flow.

This is pointing, but the finger is not an instruction. So release the notion of understanding what's going on. Just drop it. And just flow wherever my questions take you. Do not calculate like in chess—"oh, this is where she is going with this..." Blah, blah. Drop it.

Charles: I don't know if this is helpful, but I am questioning some of my beliefs about enlightenment. I just let my mind flow and wrote down these fantasies.

What does enlightenment mean to me?

- It means freedom from all that I consider to be bad in me.
- It means I will not have to do any more work.
- Everything will work out to my advantage from that point onward.
- It will be a final and everlasting solution to all my life problems.
- It means I will be looked upon with reverence.

- It means I am someone very special, and it's better if only I get it.
- It will lose some value if everyone else also gets it along with me.
- It is a kind of master self-improvement project.
- Hmm, in short it means exchanging my defective/broken self for this Super-Self

Even as I write, these ideas sound very stupid, but somewhere deep down I have been secretly holding them I can see the uselessness of living a life from a perspective of a self. Maybe these ideas also act as a block. I need to question myself about my ideas of enlightenment.

Elena: That was really honest. That's fantastic. That's moving away from the cartoon ideas of this, clearing out the caricatures and childish thoughts. This is getting real, and the more real you get, the easier it is to see. Now you've looked at these reasons, can you see where that self is hiding?

Yes, in your "spiritual advancement and benefits" fantasies.

Enlightenment is nothing more than seeing that self is an illusion. No angels, no magic wand erasing all your troubles, no people around you seeing a halo around your head and respecting you and all that, as you rightly observed.

It is so simple. When you really look and see that you are not there, just life living of its own accord, you will laugh.

They call it "the cosmic joke"—like every man should just look honestly behind all the assumptions, simply look at reality, and be able to see the truth. Why do you think it's not happening with everyone? Because self is playing this game, hiding in any way it can. Like yours. I'm sure many spiritual seekers could say exactly the same, if only they looked honestly.

So look. Who is driving life? What's really going on when you say "I"?

"I" is a label that points to nothing. Is this true?

Do not answer from your beliefs; LOOK.

Charles: I looked around in the room to see what I see, what is real. I saw many real things, then I looked at myself in the mirror, and a thought came to me: "this is real, my body is real".

I realised then, yes, the body is real, but the statement that my body is real is a lie.

Elena: Yes.

Where is this "my" that claims the body? There is only this body. It is real, but where is that part which the thoughts label as "My Body"?

The body is real, yes. It exists. "Mine" is just a label—but unlike the label "body", the label "mine" doesn't refer to anything that is real.

See if this is true. Find "you". Find out if "you" is real, if it exists or if it's just a label we wear so long that we forget it's not there. Look.

Charles: Thanks for your help and patience. I am trying to be on it as much as I can.

When I got up today and was brushing my teeth, I tried to check this out. Initially there was a sense of doing, the thought/mind statement was "I am brushing", but as I focused more on it no I was in place. It seems that this "I thought" is a part of every thought itself.

I know there is no Batman, and I do not live my life as if there is a Batman there. But even though I know there is no self here at all, the problem is that, even after not being able to find the self anywhere ever, these thoughts that assume self keep arising and I keep getting identified with them.

This process is definitely helping me. There are a few things that have shifted for me. I am no longer expecting a big bang event for the realisation, and have also got over the silly grandeur about life after the realisation. I guess I will be OK with the ordinariness of life.

I would love to live life the way you guys describe it. It sucks to be trapped in this illusion of self. I just want to experience being in the flow of it. Anyway, all these are just assumptions on my part, for now.

A strong sense of "I" has come up for me. It is the "I" that controls or directs the attention. I am honestly not able to say that attention just happens; it feels that it is being directed (cause and effect). Like I think to myself "I will raise my hand", and I do it, i.e. raise my hand.

Elena: Yes. The fiction of 'I' is indeed part of every thought. And it will always be. This is not about purging identity—that's impossible, and ties people in horrible knots. It's the classic trap for all seekers, to expunge identity. It's impossible, identity just reforms around that effort.

All this is, is seeing the truth that NO identity can EVER refer to anything real, because there actually is no you.

Do you understand? Stop trying to purge identity. Instead, see that there is nothing behind it.

And yes, it does indeed suck to be trapped in the illusion of self.

Now release your expectations. They are holding you back from seeing the truth, because you've been taught to look for something huge, mystical and ephemeral.

The actual reality that there is no you is none of these things. It is real, simple, immediate, and quite pedestrian, in and of itself.

Drop, drop these assumptions. You are losing focus because of the 100% focus on looking, build up the intensity. Something is holding you back. See what's holding you back. Ask. Listen.

What is holding you back? What? What is holding you back?

Better still ask—what is being HELD back? What can be? Don't just throw these questions into your mind and hope—actually search for the real answer. And get it.

Ask yourself in desperation. Become very quiet. Just sit. The answer is there—find it.

Writing is great—but make sure you cut through bullshit relentlessly. Do not spare any little corner.

I will stay with you until you're done, regardless of how long it takes. And one never knows. Just trust the flow.

Charles: I think I've got it. Or should we say lost it?

My guess is that what finally triggered it was an instruction about my meditation sits. I was told to "just observe the thoughts, but there is no need to obey the contents of the thoughts, they are just thoughts arising and not commands to be obeyed." Reading this, what you all have been trying to say fell in place.

The "I" thoughts will still keep arising, but there is no need or compulsion to believe in it or buy into their story anymore. For me, no big shifts or big bangs or anything, just this realisation. The "I" thought arises, just like all other thoughts, but giving it energy by engaging in it is what makes it important.

This is a big realisation, but I don't know about enlightenment. Actually, does not matter either way. At the least this illusion of self/I/me/mine is seen through. If this is all there is to enlightenment, then so be it. If there is something more, then at least this is done.

Once again, a Big Thanks for your efforts (I know there is no "you", but still). If you need to post our e-mail interaction anywhere publicly, please remove my real name. You may use any other alias of your choosing.

Elena: Hey, friend! Yes, that's it. YES.

Even it does not feel grand, you will see with time how it will all unfold. It will. Life will be lived just like before, but you will notice that everything will become less sticky, so to speak, not much weight. See, when we go with Vipassana and prune, prune and prune sankaras, the root is still in place. The root is identification with a separate structure—self.

So the one who was doing and striving and seeking is the self itself. Even "self" is Life itself too, until Life does not need to "pattern" itself as the self anymore. I hope you understand what I wrote. But it doesn't matter. All is available to you.

Years of watching impermanence—anicca—brought you to direct seeing to see anatta. Now what? You know: just go chop wood, carry water, as they say about enlightenment. Oh, and... if you want to thank me for this, it is better for all if instead, you pay it forward by helping others see it.

Please keep in touch! Would love to be your friend. Your honesty was outstanding.

Tom

It took a long time for Tom to realise that "I" is just a label. He has long experience with meditation. But realisation does not require meditation, and for many, although it seems extremely strange to say this, meditation can be an obstacle. But no obstacle is that great, because it's simple, to just look at what is. In the end he was working so hard and so intensely that resolution came through a dream. That was a unique turning point for Tom.—I. C.

Tom: Where am I? Physically, Germany, mentally... pretty down on all the dharma logic, believe that the "I" is a label applied to an ephemeral concept that exists only as a thought. I can't help thinking that my thinking is getting in the way of really internalising this belief into direct knowledge/realisation. How is that?

By the way, thanks in advance!

Ilona: OK, believing that "I" is a label is an accurate belief—but you really want to see the reality of it. Let's look deeper into that so there is no belief, but the seeing of the reality of it.

Please examine the word "I" closely. What does it point to? Is there any such thing in the real world? Please answer with full honesty and when you are 100% sure. Take your time.

Tom: "I" is a word and a thought pointing to the doer and experiencer of everything in my memory. I know the argument that it is irrelevant, and superfluous and an invention—I even believe the argument, but the experience seems only intellectual to me, not basic and gut-hitting.

Ilona: Ok, Tom, let's look again. The thought "I" is pointing not to the doer, but to other thoughts about the doer. There is no doer.

Look again. Examine the label "school". What does this label point to? Is there such a thing as a school in real life? There are buildings, students, books, classes, teachers… are any of them "school"? Or is it just a word that we use for communication so we can understand each other?

Can you look now at the word/label "I" in the same way? What does it point to?

Tom: OK, we're on the same page. Your precision is good and helpful. You are right, when I examine the doer, there are just stored thoughts about the doer. So "I" is a thought about thoughts, understood. Your school analogy is clear. Just a word, an agreement about a concept.

Ilona: Great! Next, have a look at how labelling works:

"I breathe", rather than "breathing happens". "I digest"—"digestion happens", "I run"—"running happens", etc. Can you see that the thought "I" is just a word that we put in front of other words in language?

There is no breather. There is no thinker. There is no watcher. There is no observer, but these are all experiences happening in one moment.

Now look inside and notice: what are the labels that you seem to identify with? Examine those.

Tom: I know this teaching, again intellectually, using the passive form instead of the involving form. It seems to bring me closer but doesn't push me off the cliff. For example, some of the things on your list have a deeper element of volition associated with them: running as opposed to digestion.

When I focus on "I", I try to see what agendas might be there and see images of myself with subtitles such as:

"Mighty meditator". "Seen as exceptionally good human". "Superhuman". "The right party in the divorce". "The good parent". "The smart big brother". "The enlightened partner". "Property owner". "The 'one' who did it".

How is this?

Ilona: Hmm, sounds like you are a lot of things. But is there a "you", really?

What if I told you now that there is no self at all in real life? None, as in zero. Describe what comes up.

BTW, do not worry; the shift is already happening with every question answered. It's also very tiny, so you may not even notice exactly when it unfolds. Just take the steps I'm asking you to and trust the process. Cool?

Tom: Very, very, very cool! I trust the process more than I trust myself!

I believe it when you tell me that there is zero self in real life. Nevertheless, there is still this "feeling" that every experience is wrapped in a cellophane package of "I". I can't see it, but it colours all of experience with this "I" flavour and objectifies it. That reinforces the "I".

To answer your question directly: I believe it but don't know it or see it. The purity of what I expect is tainted with the obviousness of subject and object, i.e. me/it.

Ilona: Time to rip that cellophane! Read this and then do it. Close your eyes. Find that which is always here. Notice the space, notice the awareness being aware, breathe and just stay with it.

Notice how thoughts appear in awareness, and don't pay so much attention to what they say. Just notice it as a baffling noise, as thoughts labelling whatever experience is noticed. Just never-ending labelling.

Notice that "I" is not anything else but just a passing thought. Just a word. See that presence/being is impersonal, but thoughts make it appear otherwise. Now check if this is true:

Is there a "you" thinking or just thoughts flowing by themselves without a thinker?

"I" is a thought. Thought cannot think. It's just an expression of processes going on in the brain.

Notice that there is no noticer, but noticing happening, that there is no focuser, but focusing happening. That there is no one to see, but seeing is happening all by itself, effortlessly.

Let me know what you find.

Tom: A little over one hour sitting under the moon. Stuck to your instructions pretty well, noticing thoughts appearing. Noticed the labelling tendency, usually shortly after the label, noticed how the thoughts tended toward reinforcing some aspect of a self. Not many unfamiliar thoughts, more like repeated patterns, future planning, stupid things which would be great once this no-self business was in the bag.

Kept reinforcing/reintroducing the thought of the absence of an "I" or self and tried to "feel" that. Sometimes that led to a growing intensity to "realise" it instead of just believing it.

Did one short exercise where I pictured my body on a moonlight cliff, stuffing pictures representing "I" thoughts from the past into a suitcase, and shoving it into the gleaming ocean below.

I'm still here. Will head to bed but try to stay clear on the goal.

Ilona: OK, cool. So what is it that kept reinforcing, reintroducing thoughts of an absence of "I"? Was that not just another thought appearing and disappearing? All by itself, just like other thoughts? What is behind the "introduced"?

No need to get rid of the "I" thought, it's just a pattern of language! Instead, look at what it really is—a thought. Does thought think?

Tom: A VERY good question. Yes. I would usually automatically say "volition", meaning "I chose that as MY theme and I'm introducing that thought due to determined effort." But, in fact, yes, it's just another thought bubbling up from the abyss.

During the sitting, this phrase/thought came up: "thought does not think, it is just a thought bubbling up". This did not seem to provide a lot of traction, though. Sometimes, I feel as though I can penetrate only so deeply into a theme and then things get hazy, and this seems to fit that pattern.

OK, I wasn't trying to "get rid" of the thought of "I Am", but used the mental phrase of "There is no self" in an almost mantra-like way to keep the focus on the exercise.

Ilona: Great! You are getting there. Now look at the feeling. Is there a feeler, or are the feelings all just passing by like thoughts?

"I am" is a clear sense of being. One that always is here now.

Thought does not think, yes! So what is going on? Can you describe what you see?

Tom: So… took a while to get to sleep, as I was trying to keep the watching of the arising of thoughts and labels alive. Woke up this morning and, while still in the wake-up haze, checked out the "I" and "self" status. Still present. But I drilled down into the thoughts and tried to keep the awareness on their spontaneous nature.

They definitely seem to be directed, orchestrated. The base assumption has always been that "I" am the director. The drive to get this done—is it habit? The universe working through this body-mind? The thoughts are too directed to be random, so there is intelligence there. I am trying to focus on the qualities and they just keep on coming: out of my control and just happening.

As I woke, I was working with these mental acknowledgements: "In seeing, just the seen." "In hearing, just the heard." "In feeling, just the felt." Etc.

It feels good and right, trying to take the "me" out of the equation of reality. It feels as though I am waiting for this sense of "I AM" to either dissolve or to clarify in some way which still eludes me.

I am trying not to expect any great firework-like shift in perception. I feel as though I may be slowly eroding a mountain of habitual "I-ing".

Question: you wrote "'I am' is a clear sense of being. One that always is here now."

Are you saying that so that I will understand what has to be seen clearly to eliminate that sense?

Ilona: The sense of being is not going to vanish. Nothing is going to change. It already is as it is. What drops is the belief that "I" is the orchestrator. And nothing drops it. It just falls away when the truth is seen.

In seeing there are the seen, the seer and the seeing—as one. There are no separate parts.

In hearing—the hearer, the heard and the hearing—as one. There are no separate parts.

In orchestration... What is there?

The Universe is working not through, but as. It's expressing itself in different forms, not through different forms. What do you see there?

Tom: Just had a phenomenal sit. Maybe a shift. Lots of dharma type ideas coming up such as "the 'I' is just unnecessary flypaper hanging in the corner; sticky ugly nothing I want to relate to".

I had the impression of attention as an ocean wave, continuously rolling, not breaking... until the self felt impelled to label the data stream. So keeping attention on that cusp, just before labelling happens, seemed to be a good, if tricky, place to hang out. The feeling of a comfortable, non-clinging continuity of experience seemed possible there.

Near the end of this sit thoughts of success started to arise. This was seen but effort was needed to ensure that it would not congeal into "my success". Definitely, though, a feeling of the right direction of effort was felt as well as a general non-stickiness to the phenomena. Very pleasant.

The "I" is definitely still present; the "self" still has a strong heartbeat but I believe it's a little slower than yesterday. I am not sure how much I will be communicating this weekend as my little place in the woods is offline, but I intend to give this exercise my full attention the entire time. So don't feel a slave on my account.

Please know that I deeply appreciate your engagement so far.

You asked "in orchestration... What is there?"

There is order and intelligence. But I will allow that assumption to be just a thought about being "used to" experiencing the flow of events as something comprehensible and ordered. Clearly there are natural principles at work; perhaps order is just seeing patterns.

Then you wrote/asked "the Universe is working not through, but as. It's expressing itself in different forms, not through different forms. What do you see there?"

Hmm... I don't know. Obviously, lots of sense objects, all with organisational mind-made labels attached to them.

In my last sit, as I mentioned, I was attempting to ride a perceptual wave and experience all sense inputs as just that, sort of at the "pre-labelling" phase of arising. Right track? Coincidence?

Sitting again, another long peaceful sit. Things which normally would have been annoying, dogs barking, neighbours setting up outdoor stuff... just interesting sounds. An aeroplane flying overhead, stripped of labels or of attachment, became a peaceful droning focus of contemplative awareness. Really, really nice.

Despite the recent experience of not wanting to sit and meditate for long stints, last night's sit was long, focused and pleasant. This morning as well and just now... at least an hour each time... less and less "self"-involvement, to hazard a hope, noticing phenomena and then at first consciously detaching, then later just noticing the nature of the sounds or of the touch etc.

I would say that this is AT LEAST a right track if not THE right track. Will try not to consolidate these experiences into anything. Will try to stay aware of the "I" feeling/attachment. Will try to remain objective.

Ilona: I see you have your special way of doing it. That's cool, but seeing through illusion has nothing to do with meditation. Just like realising that Frodo Baggins is not real has nothing to do with meditation. He actually isn't real, in real life.

There is no self at all in real life, like there is no Batman and no pink elephants.

This is where I like you to look now. Which words are pointing to real things in life that exist, and which words point to fiction?

"I" is fiction. The chair, the table, the monitor, the body, the tree, the cat, the cabin and the Sun are real. Even the mind is real, as a mind. But Tom is fiction.

Please practise this exercise and report when you are ready.

Tom: Tom IS FICTION!?!? How could you say that? ... Just kidding. I'm on it!

As to your point about not having to do with meditation: that is just how I "look" deeply. It is not an altered state of mind but just a quiet place to examine my mind. If it is outside of the parameters of the method, though, I will simply look, no problem.

I did the exercise as you prescribed. As before, the intellectual aspect of this is very firm. I "know" that there is not and never has been an "I" or a "self" as some independent entity observing or controlling or mediating this reality.

There may have been a subtle shift, a deepening of this knowledge, but no great "AHA!" experience. It seems to be a slight change of perspective. I will remain on this until I am 100% sure. I WILL get this done.

Are there any markers that this knowledge is more than just intellectual that I should be looking for?

Ilona: Yes, the shift is very subtle, no gongs, no angels singing, no bright lights in the eyes. Just the falling away of belief, which happens when you see the actual truth of this.

Can you describe what you see? What is Tom? With full detail, please.

Tom: So I should ignore the gongs and angels? OK.

"Tom" seems to be a habit of identification more than a concrete entity; a viewpoint which I have not yet managed to shake off. It is always as though "I" am looking, or "I" am hearing, and therein is already the "I" identification.

When I focus on hearing, for example, I can listen to birds and the rush of distant traffic and "drop" the label-making habit, so that perception is "riding the wave" of the sound at a "crest" BEFORE the label ("bird" or "traffic") is applied. Nevertheless, it seems always to be "looking out" from a certain viewpoint.

The experience doesn't exactly emulate "in the seeing, just the seen" kind of description. There is separation. Does this help?

Ilona: I'd like you to look at Tom from a slightly different angle. It's a character. A real character with likes and dislikes, but it's fictional. There is a story unfolding and Tom is the hero of it, like Batman.

What do you see now?

Tom: I see the character, the stories, the dramas, the story line. The intimate details are known; pictures of the character, from the past, typing now. Memories are just thoughts, pictures are thoughts too—reinforcing reality of the character...

Trying to see the character as transparently "unreal" as I see Batman. But "I" am still looking.

Ilona: Good, you see the character, nice. Now let's go back to the "I". "I" is a thought. Thought does not think. Is this true?

Examine thinking with thinking. How does it happen, what influences it, where do thoughts come from?

What do you see?

Tom: Clearly, "I" is a thought. It is also clear that thought does not think. The mechanism of how thoughts come about is unclear and probably, for this exercise, unimportant. But one thought seems to condition another, to colour it.

But yes, "I" is only a thought. The thought itself does not think.

When I try to follow your instruction of "examine thinking with thinking", thinking seems to stop. I focus in on the thought process and it is either held in abeyance or seems foggy, hazy, impenetrable.

Ilona: OK, so we are clear that thought does not think. So tell me, who is focusing? Is there anything behind it, doing the focusing? What is looking?

Tom: Here's the tricky part. I know the answer is that "no one" is focusing, focusing is just happening. But it still feels as though focusing must be initiated by "something". All of my life the simple answer was that "I" was that something.

My body just went for a walk with the hounds. During the walk, while being assailed by thoughts of thought arising on its own, suddenly recollections of a couple of "past life regressions" popped into awareness. I compared the recollection of those experiences with some of those which in this life I call mine. It is VERY VERY clear that there is not even the slightest difference in substantiality between those "past life" "I"'s and this life's "I"'s. So the fact that all is thought, nothing else, is very clearly seen.

The present experience, happening now, flowing by, is still objectified. Is this separation between me experiencing and experience just happening something that will suddenly disappear, or will it gradually wear away if seen in the light of this "no self" perspective?

Is it expected that the perception of the flow of experience will no longer be encumbered with an "I"?

Thanks for putting up with me!

Could that "something which initiates" simply be a "pattern", a habitual way of thoughts arising that I associate with me?

Ilona: Your message made me smile.

When you see that "I" is just a label and that the mind's function is to label experience, the thought "I" becomes empty. With that realisation, there is no more middleman attached to experience. Life is; things happen. They don't happen to you, but as you.

Now look very closely at this and tell me what comes up inside: there is no self at all in real life.

Check within. Is this true? If not, what is the feeling there?

Tom: That rings true. There is no self other than the thought label and the residue of decades of habit. It is obviously so. The middleman function is also clear and clearly unnecessary.

The feeling which comes up upon that query is a little like a giddy freedom feeling.

Ilona: Initiation happens as a result of subconscious processes. An "itch and scratch" kind of thing. The brain gets information through the senses and makes decisions based on what is happening. This goes through the filters of beliefs, and labelling happens as result.

Look at your dogs. What initiates their behaviour?

Tom: Food!

Ilona: Hahahahaha! Yum. But they also feel love and express it freely, without labelling. There are no worries in a dog's head.

OK, how about a human?

Oh, yes, the feeling of freedom inside! It's great to know that life is happening and relax as it works fine without a general manager of the universe.

Tell me, what do you see when you look at humans?

Tom: Hmm… no idea how deeply a dog thinks or where the reaction stops. Obviously, they have patterns which they follow. Far less complex and driven by strategy than a human's, but there is thinking going on there.

People label, they build labels into templates and navigate their reality via those already-digested templates of reaction. Humans… self-obsessed, worried beings, largely living out of sync with the present. Planning for the future, regretting the past, calculating advantage and disadvantage in millisecond tact. Missing out on experience by filtering it or relying on the shortcut of stored reactions.

Ilona: Yes, life for a human = suffering. All because of the unexamined assumption that "I" is an entity.

So are you through? Do you have any questions? Is everything crystal clear?

Tom: I really can't say that I am. I would like to sit with this a while and get back to you. Examine it, live with it and deepen it. If I have any questions, I hope you don't mind if I come back to you. But I will let you live your conventional life again, and me mine.

Thank you for your kindness and efforts. If I can help you in any way please let me know without hesitation.

Ilona: That is good idea—to let it sink in. From what I see, the shift has already happened, you just need to let it unfold. There is nothing left to do but to relax and notice the obvious. Please feel free to ask anything at all and report back when it feels right.

If there is a feeling of stuck-ness, it's best to address it and work through it rather than not.

Tom: I believe it when you tell me that there is zero self in real life. Nevertheless, there is still this "feeling" that every experience is wrapped in a cellophane package of "I".

Ilona: Well, again Tom—I'm not asking you to believe me. I'm asking you to check. You cannot agree your way free. You have to actually look.

I see that you have been anchored in the real world. That is great.

So who/what is experiencing the real world? Is there an experiencer? Does life need an experiencer to be present?

Can you look deeply at the real world? Is there anyone controlling what is happening? Can you see that mind labels, and that thoughts like "yes, it's me" are just thoughts passing by? And that this, too, is happening by itself?

Is it true that there is no controller? Is it true that life is just happening by itself? Please answer when you are ready.

Tom: "I" is the invisible, untouchable security blanket wrapped tightly around this idea of self. My seeing is still through the weave of this blanket. I know this but don't feel the detachment I'm expecting from the genuine realisation of this obvious fact.

I'm still working on it. I do seem to feel a shift within which makes the mundane less important somehow; less able to cause me grief. I'm trying to see whether this is a change in perspective or relief after a few weeks of high everyday stress.

Ilona: Hahaha! "I" is a security blanket.... hmm... nope! The fear surrounding "I" is the security blanket. It's fear of exposing the fraud. "I" is not real and all your life you felt certain that it was. So look at it from this angle, and see what the worst is that could happen if "I" was exposed as a lie.

It is. A lie.

The shift is happening; it's not one moment, but a process in time, lasting a few days. Notice that.

Tom: Thanks, gotcha. I believe that a shift is underway. I am working on it and will look at it again more deeply as soon as I can. A report will follow.

P.S. During my contemplations, while looking, I have tried to see the "fear", "confusion" and hazy unclear ideas as the camouflage hiding this self. There was no event that could be described as a sudden breakthrough to clarity or dissolution of the concept of "I".

Ilona: Clarify "hazy ideas". Identify the fear. The fear is a feeling inside the body. What is it protecting? Answer this: what would be lost if it was true that there is no self at all? Look deeper and answer when ready.

Tom: Just before bed last night, I was applying your last instruction and giving myself suggestions to continue the investigation as I slept. I woke at around 03:00 from a dream in which the following occurred:

I (and some others in the dream) we're all carrying around oven trays with cakes in them. Mine had my name on it. It was "I". I had, in the dream, the very distinct knowledge that I understood clearly that the "I" was just a label pointing to nothing.

I realise that this is not how one should "investigate". Nevertheless, the dream was profound and, I believe, is the result of a deeper internalisation of this understanding. I'm a pretty grounded person, and as such don't ascribe much meaning to the literal aspects of dreams, but the "knowledge" was palpable upon awakening, and for me the salient point is that this "quest" is embedded in the mind-stream.

Parallel to my dream life, I am continuing to look at the "I" and chase the feelings the investigation churns up. I feel as though I have "let something go" over the last few days. Things are lighter, smoother, less jagged. The vicissitudes of life seem interesting, without "me" feeling as though I am being sucked into and controlled by them.

Ilona: Wow. That is a first dream liberation. Nice. Awesome dream.

See, mind is resolving the confusion by itself. There is no "how it should be"; it works in the way that's best for you. And if this knowing comes from a dream, that is how it's delivered for you.

Great! So "I" is a label. In waking life, what is the "I" that is looking at the "I"? If "I" is a label, can it look? Or does looking happen by itself?

You are getting very close...

Tom: I agree that something is happening. There seems to be more space between experience and the sense of an "I".

I don't know whether I adequately expressed the sense in the dream that "it was already my state", and that the "cake pan" with "me" in it was like a leftover which couldn't quite be dropped yet. But the base sensation was that the knowledge was there and was the experience.

"I" is definitely a label. The concept of everything happening by itself is not yet gut-level. It is understood, but the hangover of over fifty years of leaning on the lie is still present, although definitely attenuated.

Ilona: Your word "hangover" made me laugh. LOL. Yes, that's how it can be described.

Can you look at Tom again and see what you find now. What is Tom? How does it operate? Is there a driver inside the body?

Tom: No. Just driving.

Ilona: Rant about it, please. What is Tom?

Tom: At the moment, the body is working, so the attention given to the question is limited. Nevertheless:

Tom seems more transparent than before. Less important. Still seems to be the experiencer to a degree, though, despite my clearly seeing the now obvious fact that this can't be. While trying to delve into the feelings of fear/attachment to the idea of "me" yesterday, there were only subtle feelings to track, difficult to see.

Some pointing to a latent desire to "be seen as the 'morally right' person" in some old mental baggage situations. This insight made me laugh to see how I was still churning through decades-old themes and holding them as mine, and being attached to some possible future judgement about them. Then, later, the dream.

Ilona: That's it. You're through. I can see that you are through! Welcome to the flow! Thank you very much for looking. It was a pleasure from my side to assist you.

From now on, liberation starts, and all beliefs are going to fall. Like dominoes. The key is to inspect everything, acknowledge it and release it. When stuff comes up and it feels like something is not right, always look inside. There will be something that wants to hold on, especially to the precious beliefs close to the heart.

Well, it's a journey without a driver, so Tom can relax and enjoy! I'm delighted for you.

Just for the end bit, what was that click that pushed it through, what was that last push?

Tom: From my side I would not say yet that I am through, but there is no impatience connected with this. Perhaps it is the writing style or the inherent imprecision of communicating concepts, but your confidence is not yet shared. As before, I will take your advice and observe and let go.

To answer your "end bit" question, the dream was very compelling, it was such a strong sense of knowing that the message was GOTTEN. Will keep on reality check, though.

I will check back occasionally and let you know how it progresses.

I thank you for your guidance and wisdom! Your drive to help others is obvious and cherished.

Ilona: I know there is still stuff to work out. Many people assume that the only hallmark of liberation is total peace. This is a cartoon idea of what liberation actually is. It's just the real seeing of the actual reality of the unbroken, uncaused flow of life. And that line has been crossed.

It helps to look at what the doubt is and what's behind it; check there! Write to me until it's all clear.

Deepening is going to take some time, yes, until all beliefs are inspected and released. All I want to know is if you have seen it clearly, or not.

Was there ever a self?

Tom: No there was never a self. Again, my dreams were clearly pointing to a deep realisation of no self. The knowledge is being internalised and the habits worn away.

This morning's meditation was largely taken up with being present with all arising phenomena, with the focus on everything just arising and passing away. No self, no "I" other than the labelling process... all sounds just being there, requiring no intercession of a "me".

It still requires a conscious effort, but is each time it becomes easier, which is interpreted as "less self" in the way. It is becoming easier to take the less egoistic view that these thoughts, and the direction or tendency toward realising no-self, are just emerging from some depth beyond "me", not requiring "me". So I'm trying to keep "me" out of the way.

Thanks.

Ilona: Awesome, Tom, this is it. Really. And it doesn't start with all the peace—it starts with the truth. This is just the beginning, just the gate. But yes, you are now liberated, that's what it means. The actual seeing that you've done, that's the permanent shift. You made it through.

It's a bit like a hangover after realisation. It takes some time to release all that is left hanging in there without a centre to attach to.

I'm delighted for you. Truly. It fills my heart with huge appreciation. Thank you.

May I use it for my blog? It really helps people. Makes it easier for them to see. It's great to cover it from many angles, and yours is valuable as it shows how it can also happen through a dream! Powerful stuff.

Tom: Of course you can use it for your blog. It's funny that the dreams played a role, as they historically haven't done so in my life.

As before, I see the realisations which I have had to this point only as stepping stones. The way all of this plays out interests me. Observing reactions in stressful situations is always a very good base to measure progress in my experience. Things seem far less emotional at this point but there have been no real difficult tests as of yet.

I know that I am still capable of anger and other passions and so know that I am still tied to suffering. Since this process began, however, there has been much less clinging and reaction to charged situations. My meditation has been significantly deeper and clearer and the process just seems right and comfortable.

Thank you for your help and guidance again. Don't be surprised if my e-mail address pops up occasionally with a report or two.

Stay well.

Ilona: You are most welcome, Tom. Write to me any time you feel like. I love hearing from my free friends.

Lars

Lars is professional artist and painter from the Netherlands who has exceptional skill with the use of light. I saw his work on the Internet and wrote to him just to say how much I appreciate his paintings, when he suddenly said he read my blog and would like me to guide him. He was searching for enlightenment and had a guru. We connected right before his scheduled retreat, and... well, you'll see. After he released the last bit of the illusion, new creativity was unleashed and many more works of art came to life. They are of unprecedented beauty.—E. N.

Lars: Hello, Elena.

The search is in its last months; it's very intense.

There is no self/Lars to find, it seems so clear... yet there's a blind spot: the thought comes up that I have to go through a door to make the shift. That brings me to the thought: no way, because then you project in the future!

So I guess there's an understanding on the rational side, yet there are moments of no-self. Afterwards the thought comes up: "where was I"?

Also, there's the feeling I'm conceptualising the Advaita pointers too much; too much thought.

When I paint or make music there's no self, but there should be no self in all activities.

Can you help me, Elena? Please ask anything you want to know! I'm online every day, except 25-28 august, when I'm at a retreat.

Elena: You saw that the self does not exist when you paint or you play—it's just movement—the vibrational movement of creation. Who cares what form it takes?

Now you need to show the mind this realisation. What happens is that you fall into the no-self state when you start painting, and you have no idea how you got there, and the mind is not registering what's going on. A hallmark of the no-self state is no thinking—just flow.

What you need to do is to point the mind to this. How? By comparing what is real and what is imaginary. This has nothing to do with the no-self state. So you need to look at reality as if you'd just been born, freshly. Does a baby have a self when it opens its eyes and moves to its mother's breast? Or are there sensations and feelings of hunger, and then the body moves?

When you feel inspiration and move to take the brush and you become a brush, a song, is there a manager to this movement in Creation?

Look in this direction—look if Life requires an entity to perform actions, or if actions are movements in consciousness/creation.

See that "I" is just a thought that comes after the experience, action, and grabs the experience and creates an owner, imaginary owner—"I" breathe. I breathe? Well, when you are asleep do you do breathing or is it just breathing happening?

Life patterning in breathing.

Life patterning in drawing.

Life patterning, Life happening as music, as playing, as bodying, as sensations-ing, as feeling, as thinking...

There are no nouns, only verbs.

Look. Take a deep good look at what's really going on.

Lars: I never know when I start painting or doing anything else. The realisation that when I wake up the world is starting in ME is such a mind blowing reality that indeed through thought there is the false creation of a me/I so I can say: "I'm awake and it's Saturday".

What you say about open eyes, YES! It feels like I see the world anew every time. Every morning I go to work (home care in a hospice, place where people come to die, mostly due to cancer), I look and everything is different, different colours, people, different everything!

And then there's the thought: all this, all these people on feet, bikes, cars, metro are that one consciousness, through the illusion of separate entities. This I see very clearly!

Is there a manager in the movement of creation? Always thought there was, these days I'm about to say NO, there's not. This changes the whole idea of the Artist and his inspiration! HAHA bullshit!

No, If you ask me why I started painting in 2003 I just can't answer. I was doing something with Japanese tea bowls and felt the urge to make some drawings, and there it was, seriously. The next year I stopped working (full time indoor sales) and was a student at the art academy.

This just happens, finding a gallery, and now the second one. It just happens; there is no "I" who can control anything!

So what I'm going to do is take a good look at this and report back to you!

Thank you for doing this, Elena!

Elena: Look not at life in general; look at your immediate experience.

Lars: Hi, Elena.

Immediate experience is that which never stops. I can talk generally, but that is done without an "I". I think that everything is direct experience, because there is a body named Lars, and he can communicate with another body named Elena. This is my immediate experience.

There's the idea of you and me, but we are one. That's what triggered you to contact me, and that's what triggered me to work with you. That's immediate; for me it's also a direct experience.

But maybe you're referring to something else. Is there a clue you can give me about this direct experience?

The world is not the same for me, yet the world never changed. Thinking about the concept "Lars", a boyish man of 37, makes me laugh. He is a Shakespearean role on a stage. More and more I'm realising: I AM. That is not a person, it is not a self.

Immediate? Please feel free to ask me anything you want to know.

Realisation/enlightenment seems to be the last concept, the last ego projection, the Holy Grail. But!... Life, doesn't it live by itself? Elena, I can go to another guru, satsang, read another book, meditate—but isn't that a movement away from life itself?

This body... yes, it breathes, and that heart beats without effort, that brain works, and no matter what, Lars is looking: is there a do-er, is there an "I" who runs the show?

I can't find it, Elena. What is immediate is this presently sitting and typing: that is what it is right now. There are two fingers typing,

This thought comes up now: what is there beyond this? The shift? The final realisation? You know this story where there's a bar, and in the bar there's a sign: "free beer tomorrow!"

Elena, is there anything I can do? So yes, looking at the immediate, this is immediate right now: fingers typing this, thoughts arise, they disappear, the light on the table...

My body starts to relax, I'm in a sort of not-knowing, Lars is a fiction. So that which makes Lars and you and everybody else possible must be real?

And during our work, I'm not reading Advaita and not going to Facebook or forums. Looking at direct experience is what I do!

Elena: Did you ever exist?

Lars: NO. There was a body born in 1974. His parents called him Lars. Though as a direct experience, there is awareness, there are eyes that see that what moves the body is there. That is not Lars. It's not an "I".

The liberation I feel right now is that I still had the idea that I should go somewhere to get that last clue to enlightenment. Like that retreat, a future event, a Guru who says keep looking till you see. Good intentions, sure, but it's always a movement away from now. Your question about the immediate was so in tune with me being tired of looking!

Did I ever exist? I thought I did, but thought is thought, Lars is thought, the body is real, life is real, that which makes us do this is real. Persons are not; they are fiction.

So looking at the world, talking to my friends, thinking about my ex-girlfriend doing work in the arts: it's all done without a somebody doing it.

A paradox, crazy wild like being a baby again, there is freshness to everything. The amazing part is that I always knew this on some level, but the mental energy I spent on the illusion of being the person Lars was a lot.

Now it's falling away. The freshness, the beauty remains, the aliveness remains!

Elena, isn't this it?

Elena: What is the expectation? What do you expect to feel? How should it be? What should change?

Look honestly and ask. Ask. Find out. You know this. You just never asked.

So do not ask me, just ask these questions, and find the answers inside. Be absolutely honest. As if I told you that you should pull out only answers that are 100% true, otherwise there will be no ability to paint and play anymore—that type of honesty. No less.

Lars: Yes, Elena, I will ask myself this and come back to you later. Must chew on this one with complete honesty!

Elena: Good man, get back to me when you find something.

Lars: The expectation of bliss and being something else after enlightenment. But now right now I feel perfect and see that there couldn't be anything other than this. I'm not a person. I'm life itself, so it's clear! Thank you for this. You are wonderful for doing this.

Elena: Yes, life always flowed without a self, so life just continues to flow. And bliss comes not from not having problems, but from appreciating what is here right now. If one really sees that "I" is just a label for the experience, any experience is worthy of appreciation. Appreciation is bliss.

And conditioning will start to fall away because there is no glue—no "I" to protect.

Lars: Right now I am where I always have been, but it took some years to get there, and that isn't even the right way to put it: I've never been anywhere else. I was always awareness/consciousness experiencing life without a person inside. I already knew this for some time, but a thought came up with the idea I need recognition from a teacher, or you!

Working with you is the last pointer for me: I know this because I AM this! Nobody can tell me, because there is nobody! The retreat is booked so I could end up there, but even that I don't know. There is nothing I can tell about the future. I don't know!

My idea about bliss and enlightenment vanished, it's gone, the appreciation of life is something immediate, it is NOW!

HERE, THIS, THIS IS IT!

When a guru tells me about enlightenment, the right questions, bhakti, and all that stuff, I think: who is there to get enlightenment? If there's nobody there, what is the whole idea about enlightenment anyway?

Realising there's no "me" doesn't mean I should behave weirdly, or should behave coldly and without empathy. No, just be who you are, do your work, talk to people, enjoy yourself. The expression of life itself is with compassion and love but also sometimes with war and hate and anger... yes, it is like that. You think that you can be in bliss all the time? No way, there's also sadness, there's frustration and all that stuff, but without an I, those things come by like clouds, the good and the bad stuff are just clouds passing by!

So what to do with all those Advaita books? Give them to others who still need to read! I really don't feel like reading those books, about other people who tell me what they know, again! Instead I can read a biography of Chopin or Lucian Freud. Or a comic book, or read nothing for a while!

The beautiful thing about this is that somehow you and I (which is language of course) found each other, and in no time there was this work, and it was the last pointer, the last time I "need" to ask for help.

There is just ONE, never been any different!

So how am I right now?

Like a newborn, fresh and bit uneasy, but also what I already was. This is about losing an illusion, not gaining new spiritual information!

I've to tell my guru that I don't have any questions anymore. Not being a seeker anymore, it's crazy and super normal at the same time!

The whole idea that made me a seeker was that I thought there was something to find. Realising there's no "I" to begin with, then there's nobody to get enlightenment, and seeing this makes that all the questions burn away. And what is left? Life itself, Lars is part of life, Lars is life, life continues itself without effort, paintings will be painted, and the rest.

This is how I feel right now, Elena!

You're wonderful just the way you are!

Elena: Wow. Perfect. Describe it further, you have a way with words.

Lars: The nakedness, freshness of every moment, no self, thoughts come by, no problem, subtle changes come by, people look at me, strangers give me a smile, my body relaxes, I feel like a newborn, and yet everything is the same, no fireworks, just being here!

See that there is just one!

Oh, and as a last note? Today I called "my" "guru" and said "there are no more questions". He said "OK, that's fine..." Looks like I don't need to go the retreat then! Never had a clue it would be today!

Chandi

Chandi had a problem with focusing. Even though she had a strong intention to look, something kept distracting her. Her mind was creating all kinds of diversions to keep her from finding out what was really going on. The turning point was when she started to chase those distractions to the source. It was quite beautiful when she saw it.—I. C.

Chandi: Hi, Ilona.

I've been really and honestly considering the possibility that there really is no me. Been trying to look at different angles, seeing when I react to other people, and then trying to see WHO is reacting. And basically what comes up is that I really can't find a someone called Chandi.

When I have no thoughts, or when I look for the "solid entity-ness" of Chandi, I can't find it. It is usually a thought which makes whatever emotion or thought "mine". But, Ilona, that happens after the fact. Like I react at the time, being caught up in the illusion of "me" and my emotions, so to speak, and then afterwards realise that the "me" was actually not really there. It is yet another thought saying so.

I'm now looking into responsibilities and their ownership. That which makes me panicky. What do I do now? All the millions of things which need doing, presumably by me, for my kids, father, work, etc., etc. If "I'm" not in control, then what? Who is going to do it all? I can't let go!

Ilona: All good, Chandi, the process has started.

Life is happening by itself, there is no separate doer, and there is no separate person that takes care of things. It's life itself. So don't worry, once you really see that self is not real, then nothing will change. Your kids, father, and so on are going to be taken care of. They already are, it's only a thought in your head that makes it appear as if it's you doing all these things.

In truth, there's no-one there. And there doesn't need to be anyone there for the love to be there, or the care, or the action. And that idea that there does? It's just another fear. Look behind that.

There is no central control over what is happening, as it is just happening, all by itself. There is no "you" to influence life, no need for a manager.

Reactions happen the same way as scratching follows an itch. Notice that. There is a story playing itself out. Here is the character, Chandi, that reacts in particular ways to particular stimuli. Let's not get involved in the story now. Just look deeper:

There really is no self at all in reality.

Notice how everything is already happening by itself. Notice that you are seeing it ALREADY, it's just that thoughts arise and go away that say the opposite. Do not believe the thoughts.

Notice what is happening around you, the totality. Write down what you see.

Chandi: Yes, yes, I see that, I see the mind/thoughts following a pattern with the reactions. The same things will trigger the same reactions, maybe it's conditioning over the years, but as you say, I'm not getting involved in the stories. It's a question of not believing the thoughts. But it's a powerful thought. OK.

It's hard to believe that things will happen without 'me'. Even though it is known, the fear continues. Trying to look deeper. Really, at the moment can't go beyond that. Focusing.

OK, if I am not the one, say, loving my kids, if there is no me, then where is the loving happening? Why do the love and responsibility feel so personal? Will it still be felt? Am I talking nonsense?

Ilona: It's happening in reality. As part of the flow of things. Maybe the fundamental part—love is real. But it's not happening to "you" and it's not coming from "you".

It is hard to believe that things will be happening without you. This is conditioning, unquestioned assumption. Everything is already happening without you managing or doing anything.

There is no doer at all. There is no thinker at all. Notice it now—thought appears, fingers start typing; all this is happening by itself.

Look at the fear itself. What is it protecting? Bring it closer—don't worry, it's just fear. Look at it with respect—it's doing its job perfectly. Can you see that?

Chandi: The fear is making me feel a little sick! And yes, it's doing its job well. It's protecting the illusionary Chandi from being seen through, the Chandi which is in turn supposedly protecting the people who she loves and cares for. It's actually quite funny, but so hard to let go of.

Help, Ilona. Where do I go from here?

Ilona: You don't need to get stressed about this, don't worry. So, fear is there to protect the illusion of a separate self, something 'running' the show. Look at it without trying to change the fear. Bow to it in honour of how well it does its job. See what happens now. Can you let the fear just be there?

Chandi: Ilona, I think I have to sit with this one for a while. Is it OK if I write again later to you? It's great you're taking the time/effort to do this.

Can't thank you enough. Also, want to tell you that I'm feeling super sensitive right now... noises and emotions and everything...

Ilona: I love helping people see this simple thing. Write to me when it feels right, I'll keep guiding you until it's over. Once you make peace with the fear, let me know.

Chandi: Ilona, I lost my focus. Had an extremely stressful day, and just couldn't focus internally. But I'm not giving up. I'll see it through, just need more time.

Is that OK? Again, I'm not going to give up. I'm planning a short trip to the mountains tomorrow. Hopefully it will be calmer there. I know it's all life, but sometimes one needs a little outward calm to be able to look inwards, no?

Can we keep speaking? Thanks.

Ilona, there's always so much going on in my life that it's hard to be able to sit and focus and write. I guess it's the same story with everyone, actually. But I'm trying, and the desire for truth burns as much as ever.

Ilona: Keep looking! What does the word "I" refer to? Is there anything in real life that you can find?

Chandi: I can't when I think about it. But why do I still get emotionally involved in the "I", the thoughts, the emotions? How can one understand on one level, and not practically?

Ilona: Emotions just happen. Feelings arise as a reaction to situations, but who is feeling? Feelings are, and come and go, thoughts, too, come and go. It's just the mind's function to label experience by itself.

Chandi: So what does one do, then? Keep not believing the thought which does that?

Ilona: No, you see the truth. Use thoughts to work it out, if you want. Tell me, where do thoughts come from? Can you control them?

Chandi: Nope, can't control them, they appear whether one wants them to or not.

Ilona: What is the thought "I"? What does it refer to? The thought "I am thinking" is just a thought, like "I am not thinking".

Chandi: Hmm. Yes.

Ilona: See? Now have a look at these thoughts: "There is no separate self at all." "I am a separate self."

Does one mean more than the other?

Chandi: I seem stuck, Ilona. I don't know if the "stuck-ness" is in my head, a thought, or if I really don't know where to go from here. You must be getting tired of me by now. What happens is that I can't seem to "maintain" the "no-I".

Keep getting pulled into being the self by life. When I am relaxed, I don't find the self. But it's so hard to relax, with kids and other stuff going on. Do you have children?

Ilona: Of course you can't maintain "no I". This isn't a belief you convince yourself into thinking, then maintain. It's not a training exercise where you learn to be happy. It's clear seeing that dissolves the illusion and then there is nothing left to maintain. Once it's seen through, relaxation comes naturally. It takes time to adjust, but life gets less and less stressful until nothing touches the nerves anymore.

But all this is irrelevant at the moment. You will see it for yourself. For now just answer me this: where do the thoughts come from? What drives the body? Does it need a manager?

I have no kids, only a cat.

OK, when you look at a baby, can you see self in there?

Simply answer these questions with perfect honesty. Looking forward to hearing from you.

Chandi: What to do, the conditioning goes so deep... It seems "wrong" to believe that there can be no soul driving the body-mind. It's so big in Islam, the idea of a separate soul.

And yes, when I try to trace thoughts, it seems they just come up, without a "me" controlling them. But that's when I'm actively focusing on it. My body… back and forth.

But thanks to what you told me the last time, I can see how reactions and responses just arise, without a personal self controlling them. It's like a program on a computer!

Ilona: Chandi, nothing in this challenges Islam. We are not looking for a new belief here, we want to just look for the truth and see it for what it is. The point is not "there is no soul"—there may well be—the point is that you don't own the soul. There's no you to own it. In fact, this is what the Sufis call Fana'a. The end of self.

Now look: who/what is focusing? Is there something that makes it happen or does it happen effortlessly by itself?

Is there anyone directing the focusing? Is focusing just happening?

Chandi: Is it kind of like how our bodily processes are just happening (without us being the manager): cells renewing, food digesting, breathing? And also is seeing, thinking, doing, also just happening without a manager? Your bit about focusing just happening made me realise that yes, it IS just happening effortlessly.

I'm just so used to claiming ownership of it that it happens so quickly. But yes, no director really.

Ilona: Yes! You are looking at it. Now see if you can go deeper. What is the "I"?

Chandi: Yes, Ilona! I see that!

Sorry, I must have been asleep when you wrote, as I'm in Pakistan. Not sure where you are. It's Sunday afternoon here now.

It's great. What I see of the "I" is that it's like an operating system on a computer (our 'Windows', kind of) and since it's encountered everywhere, it's believed to be our identity. Just a collection of thoughts, emotions, etc. everywhere, but we don't have to believe that they are who we are. It's there to keep the character going, but when it's seen for what it is, well, we can still use it but don't have to be identified with it.

I'm excited that I can see that, and I hope I'm seeing right, and not 'convincing my mind' of what I've heard or read. But YAY who is there to do the convincing and be convinced? There really isn't anyone, is there? Wow!

The world feels just a tiny bit different. But Ilona, what about the huge 'shifts in consciousness' and things that people talk about? It's not like that. I don't feel so different, but I do in a way. I'm seeing that everything, including me, is flowing with and as life. Every sound, every sight, everything is sacred.

How do we get so wrapped in our identities as not to see that?

Ilona: Awesome, Chandi! Yes, you are seeing it. Can you write what happened? What exactly made you see it? How did you come to this?

Chandi: Hmm. It's like I knew it, but I thought I didn't. Almost like that. A few things you said made me realise it.

Like I used to get stuck on my feelings and reactions. Like if there's no "me", then how come I reacted like that? But when you said, then I realised it really is like a computer program in a way. It's just happening. Doesn't mean there has to be a self to control, to feel, etc.

Also the point when you asked "who is the one who is focusing?" or something. And I was thinking "I have to focus to know there is no 'I'." It's like this self-perpetuating loop which got interrupted then. Who is focusing?

Shouldn't there be bells ringing or something huge? Ha ha. On the other hand, it's all like that somewhat. Thanks ever so much, Ilona. But what about later, if perhaps the identification happens again? What next? Is there a next?

Ilona: Oh, brilliant!

There are no trumpets and no medals, no angels going to sing. This illusion of separation simply falls away, and that's it. Everyone expects something big, but hey, nothing has to happen, it already is what is.

What has been seen cannot be unseen. Ever.

Next is different for everyone, but it's about bits of illusion falling like dominoes. All that has been stuck gets released, clarity grows, seeing deepens. For now, just relax, let it sink in.

Writing really helps to look into darker places to cut through illusion, so when you have time, can you write a big piece addressing what self is, what "I" is, what is real, just whatever flows?

Another thing that really helps clarify it is to work to spread it to others. It's one of the greatest things about doing this, and helping others see through the knots, is that it deepens my own insight into the truth, and therefore my freedom.

Much love, Chandi, and thank you VERY much for looking.

Elizabeth

Elizabeth had been seeking all her life, for decades, and was exhausted from the search. This woman was so intense that the first couple of days with her, I felt burning in my body. She was burning. I was burning. But I kept the Gate, kept the focus on the Gate. That's all that was needed. For some the intensity is the force that will bring them through the Gate. She has farm animals, and when we hit the wall, and I didn't know how to proceed with her, I directed her to look at her chickens and learn from them. As they say, necessity is the mother of invention. I think you'll find this useful—E. N.

Elizabeth: Hello, I would really like to work with you to get through that Gate! Are you free to do this work? My request is sincere and I am ready to crack this thing! I've done ten years' shamanism, fifteen years' motherhood, forty years' "seeking", and in the last two years dropped everything down to the bare bones to get to the truth.

I have no spiritual practices and stripped away as much of the un-truth as I can see. I can still smell the 'stink' of wrong-ness, though. I hope this makes some sense.

Elena: Hi, Elizabeth! I feel your hunger for this. Perfect. We can do it. Tell me more about the "stink of wrongness".

My "resume", by the way is close to yours. Eight years of Gurdjieff's Way, eight years of Vipassana, nineteen years of motherhood. I hear you. Heh heh.

Elizabeth: Oh, Elena, thanks for taking this on! I appreciate it. From your blog I gather that this requires straight up no-frills.

So. OK. I would like to give you a bit of back-history. I know that it isn't really what this is about, but it might explain the "stink" thing. As a kid I had the sense that everyone was pretending. And I thought it was me that was all wrong. A cynical, pedantic child...

Anyway, grew up, got into shamanism, thought I had found all the answers. I thought that the 'stink' was from people not knowing their true roots, the way the cosmos worked, all that. But then one day I got bit. Not sure how. But two things happened.

First, I was standing in the classroom (I was a teacher for twenty years) and realised it was all a big, fat lie... all pointless, as if everyone was pretending. I dropped into a hole of nothing, and, shortly after, stopped teaching.

I burned all my bridges and left teaching, left my relationship (I had been into all the deviancies you can think of to kind of work out 'the truth') and found that nothing I believed in was true. I dropped 150lbs in weight (yup, was very big before) and just disappeared from my life. I can only describe it as kind of dying for a couple of years. The only thing I could think of was that I wanted to know "the truth".

When people talk about wanting peace or bliss or whatever as a result of enlightenment, I don't get that. I just want to know the truth.

You know, I realised that is what I always wanted. I see that now. And I made the rash decision to know that at any cost... the only thing worth doing. No ambition for money, for great achievement. I just want to understand what is going on. Then, at some point, I found Jed McKenna, then Advaita and thought that these people were talking about what I was looking for.

I don't buy the idea that there is "no one truth". I reckon there is, and I want to find it because it is itching under my skin all the time. It is also losing my friends. I don't speak much because it feels as if each word is weighed under with the shit of playing this game of being human.

When friends talk about relationships or the clothes they want or which school they want their kids to go to, I can play along for a short while. After that I can't keep it up. So I spend a lot of my time with my chickens, my beehives, my kids. The "stink" that I talk about is what I think the ego is, the accumulated scripts that people run and the face they put on.

The words come out and it feels like it is coming from unquestioned beliefs. And in case this sounds sanctimonious and judgemental (will accept both those labels), I apply it to myself too.

My boyfriend tells me he loves me. I don't answer. I want to say "Who do you love? You love an idea of me". It is like there are personalities walking around out there but I "smell" them, each personality with its own flavour. But it is just that, a personality without a person.

Does this make any sense? I am not sure I am able to express this because I haven't tried before. And then I try to work it out via Advaita and I end up with the belief that my mind and body are illusory.

Then I try from another direction and end up with the body being real and the mind being real but there being no "me". Then I'm in knots again. The only thing I can say that I know for sure, that isn't someone else's hand-me-down, is that no-one is telling the truth—the play-acting goes on and I can trust my instinct on that.

I felt it in the last few years when everything went from me... anything that wasn't "true" got burned up: spiritual practice, profession, relationship, body. But trying to pick up the pieces and make sense... Hmmm...

Sorry, thought of one other thing I wanted to add... when I read liberation or enlightenment books/sites I notice that often the core idea resonates with me, but then the "extras" seem to turn away from the truth. These extras are often "God" stuff, or "Love" stuff.

As far as I can feel to be true, if there is no "me", that is the bottom line. No frills, no extras, no promises after. I really am struggling to find the words to describe this. It is as if I can smell the rat, the "wrongness", in the room, but can't see it.

Elena: Cut out the extras, just focus on penetrating the illusion. Later you will sort out what serves you or not. Now—100% focus on looking. Deal?

Elizabeth: Happy to cut out the extras. 100% focus—definitely a deal!

Elena: I read your story. You are standing right there, Elizabeth. It's a matter of staying focused with looking. Piece of cake. You had a moment of decision, and a decision for truth at all costs was made. You passed stages where people are not sure yet. You are there.

You are at the Gate. Now—look. Take the time to really look. Find out the answer—is it you who lives your life? Is it you who stepped up to the Gate? Is there a "you" in all of the story you just told? Where is "you" in all this?

Look!

Elizabeth: OK... going to look. I'll let you know how I get on. Just wanted to say that you ask these questions and I want to: read "spiritual" books, listen to Advaita audio, eat, go online, work, clean, e-mail, tidy up... *anything* except do this. And that is how I have been.

I think sometimes the seeking wants to keep seeking just to keep busy. Why would I want to avoid the thing I want most? OK... I will leave that for now. Right now I am going to commit to looking at each of those things you ask, right now. Thank you, Elena.

Elena: Stop all this, Elizabeth, drop all the distractions. Just drop it all for the short time we are together. Later you can go ahead and do whatever. But now—only honest looking, no reading. Enough.

Why would you want to avoid it?

You don't want to avoid it. There is no "you". There's just 'wanting to avoid it' hanging there, claiming to be coming from something. It doesn't—does it? Where does it come from? Is it you?

Elizabeth: OK... very tired now, but this is where I am at with it so far with the questions you asked. I am a bit ashamed of these answers because they seem so "basic" and not the "correct" answers. Urgh.

Who lives my life? My life is lived by memories, my brain, my emotions, physical commands, old routines (programming, programmes), fear, survival (mental and physical planning), desire (chemical, physical, emotional gratification), instincts.

Lots of fearful thoughts. In the story of my life I gave you, "me" is a series of events that make more story. So, mostly "my life" consists of thoughts and physical impulses—body and mind.

But I want there to be a "me" in there! Something special and different... urgh. I didn't know that. OK... the filter that makes it feel like a "me" is just a collection of experiences and conditioning—a unique cluster but not an entity in its own right, not an "Elizabeth".

You asked about "habit". No, the habit is not me. It is another cluster of reactions based on previous experience. A mix of biological and psychological phenomenon. Shit! Pavlov's dog...

Elena: Your life is lived by memories, and your brain? Who owns the memories? Who owns the brain?

Emotions arise/pass away—it's existence, just patterning. Emotions are part of reality. They are. Not yours. You are not part of reality. There is no "you".

Experiences and physical actions are just the same patterning of existence. There is no owner.

Old routines (programming, programmes), fear, survival (mental and physical planning), desire (chemical, physical, emotional gratification), instincts. Lots of fearful thoughts.

All this exists. The only thing that doesn't is you. Find out if that's true.

And you say that you want there to be a 'me' in there? No you don't. You just want to keep the uniqueness. Listen.

Uniqueness does not go away, it's a flavour of existence. All minds are unique, all souls, all hearts—but nothing owns those minds, souls or hearts.

Look, the way you hang on is because you think that you will lose something. See if that is the case.

Elizabeth: Ahhhh. There's a lot here... I can feel it loosening, unravelling. I want to stay with this, but I need to sleep now (it is late here). Thank you so much. I am not going to let this go.

OK. So, this is what I will commit to: no books, no "busy", no distractions. Focus. I'm going to print this off and get back to it tomorrow morning and feel for the answers. I have some questions about what you just said too, if that is OK with you. Thank you!

Elena: If you wake up in the middle of the night to pee, see if the "I" wakes up too or if it's just peeing. Also, when you wake up in the morning, look up like a baby before the "I" thought is there.

Good night.

Elizabeth: Good night, Elena. Will check in with the peeing thing.

Elizabeth: Hello, Elena. I've had some sleep, but am still tired. This thing is chasing me to be done with it, I think. So I looked over the last few questions again this morning, and here is my looong response.

Some of it is just "thinking aloud", but I kept it all in, in case there was anything I wasn't seeing. And some of it doesn't make logical sense. If you read through you will see some of it was a working out process.

OK, so you asked "Is there a 'you' who is ashamed? Look closer. Look behind the feeling". Here is what came back: I am not intellectual or clever enough. An old structure of self-image. The personality/self is highly attuned to fitting in, being a chameleon. I am afraid I will expose the workings of the "machine" and show that they are slow and ugly.

I look at it and it seems to be all programming and reflexes and personality patterns. And it is endless, by which I mean that the personality structure grows more branches wherever I cut it off. Beliefs accumulating and making more behaviours/feelings. It is all shit. Just leave it alone.

Does it belong to "me"—an Elizabeth entity? It belongs to the brain or a physical/mental stimulus system, just like Pavlov's Dog. A "cloud" of responses arises and then passes on. Leave them alone. Don't get dragged along with them OK... tricky... *What* is there not to get dragged along with them? An awareness of them? So there is not a "me" but an awareness?

When I look there is no actual Elizabeth, there is a unique physical appearance and a unique psychology (pattern, programmes, reflexes, conditioning) and a unique biology, but not an actual "Elizabeth". Don't all those uniquenesses make a singularity? Enough to say there is an Elizabeth-thing unlike any other (like a snowflake)? But is there a unique *consciousness* that is "me"? A unique body-mind constellation?

But... but... but... behind the shame is just more mind, endlessly spinning on, endlessly. But what watches all this and knows? Something is able to identify this. *Who* is Elena asking to look? *Who* can observe this? Life = body plus mind plus events? Ahhhhh, something opening up.

There is a unique form of existence BUT NO Elizabeth AT THE CONTROLS. A snowflake and a blade of grass are unique, but they are not growing themselves. Something here about them being interconnected though... in the grid of life... Yes, feelings are part of existence but what watches them come and go?

Yes also to your comments about "flow"... it is all changing—the body-mind "Elizabeth" thing and the "grid"/life/patterning, all changing. You asked another question that I will get back to. You said "the way you hang on is because you think that you will lose something. See if that is the case." I am going to get back to you on that. I feel like I am unravelling something but haven't got a grip on it. Thank you, Elena.

OK... A bit more. I hope this isn't too much. If you need a different pace, tell me! So, you asked about "the way you hang on is because you think that you will lose something. See if that is the case." I think the fear is that the personality will de-stabilise without an "Elizabeth".

I will end up mad. I will be outside society, *alone* in all senses. Not special (urgh), no chasing grand dreams, no hope for more/bigger/better, the abyss/void. OK, so I ask myself, is this true? Look.

There's nothing fucking in there... I am empty... *shouting* Want to cry and vomit. Mix of sadness and disgust. A big lie. It's all a pile of leaves... the wind blows and there is nothing there! I don't know where to take this. My mind is searching for something to hold onto that *is* there...

Trying to remember all the books and theories and ideas it has had from others. I could give you plenty from those but this is 100% focus and looking for me...don't want anyone else's answers... Don't know where to turn here. I am just going to sit with being empty, or rather, full of stuff that is all leaves and dust. Shit. Feels like my head and body is floating off.

Not allowing myself any other "story" or belief to fill this space right now... Feel vast, light…

Elena: Good. Now bring it back. Is there any "you" in any shape or form in reality?

Elizabeth: Is there a "soul", a special "me", directing my life? Is there an Elizabeth directing operations? I want there to be something in there...I want the divine spark to be there. There is fighting. I want to understand what there is that grew me, that animates everything. If there is no me, there must be something.

Elena: There is Life, Existence patterning in all these various ways. It always was. Nothing to lose. And it's not the rejection of a soul—it's seeing that if there is a soul, you don't own it, it just is. It is the illusion of an owner that holds the lies together.

Elizabeth: I want to choose that way—the Advaita way (I am Oneness) or any way that leaves me something in exchange... to be special, or to get to be God... Elena, all this stuff has to come out.

Elena: You will not disappear. You never were in the first place. Existence exists and always has and always will. It's only now and all exists. The only thing that does not is "you", the label, the imaginary ownership.

Elizabeth: I am finding it all here. I didn't know it was here. This bit of looking is messing with my head!

Elena: Good.

Elizabeth: Like it is pulling in two directions.

Elena: Just look for the simplicity of it, the truth of it. The division will resolve itself.

Elizabeth: In reality there is a body, there is a mind. I cannot find an "Elizabeth" separate from that which runs the show.

Elena: Of course you can't find it, it never was. It was just belief, thought. An "I" thought that attaches itself to anything in reality. See that nothing requires this "I" that separates reality into the compartments "I" and "not I". "Mine" and "not mine". No ownership the existence; it's imaginary.

You won't lose anything. There is no "you". Never was. Ever.

Look at the depth of it, the scale of it. It's simple. Truth is simple. Illusion is complicated. Look at the simple, eternal truth.

Elizabeth: Weeell, I guess I have reached my sticky bit... I am going to give you the place I have got to, but I warn you, I suspect 90% of it is shit. I've put it here so maybe you can help me find where I have blind spots. It was a thinking process so some of it is working it out on paper. Apologies for the length of it. Here goes:

I can see the block, a lot of partly-digested beliefs and many residues of magic and magical thinking. Wanting there to be "something else". Lots of ways of the old self keeping itself intact.

Stop. Just look and see what is 100% true. Discard what is not. Brain? Computer for keeping the system alive. Thoughts? Random functions of brain system and physical feedback system and stored data.

What I am searching for, the "me" essence... I look and find "mind", but that is a dead-end. The resistance is wanting there to be something else. I can give up the 'me' idea if there is something else—Life/One-ness/God, so that this avoids the emptiness. It is just fear. Something to refer to, a path to follow.

All shit. Belief wants a belief! Been here before. Going round in circles. No belief is true... there isn't even a battle. Just patterns of existence—no meaning—just life—just this, now. NO BELIEF.

Just this, life. Each pattern is unique but it is not self-animated (no self!). There is a flow of life into life into life into life—it can't be self-contained (no self!). No owner. A radical singularity with no owner—what a contradiction. Live and die—no control over that. "Elizabeth" Is a unique existence, but there is no "I" with a control of that existence.

I didn't bring myself into existence. But the fear of letting go of "I" is of letting go of control; but it will die anyway. "Die before you die". Let the "I" die. Self doesn't want to die. Big thing being asked—kill your self off. Never existed anyway. But the idea of it existing creates the illusion of control.

Krishnamurti says his big secret was that he didn't mind what happened. I am being lived. There is no "me" doing the living. Ready to die? Cut your head off! "I" want to survive at all costs. Very, very good at surviving. Permanently controlling, vigilant, responsible.

OK... getting quieter after all this shit. Think it is the "I" fighting itself! Just look... focus... Think maybe I have to clear all this stuff out of the way. I write it and see it for what it is. Clear seeing of it, just still attached to it. Hope that makes sense. Good at seeing the shit, just less good at letting go. Maybe not very brave... Focus. "It is all just life. Happening." Everything else is a story.

Yes. Yes. I *know* this.

Elena: I see you are good at fighting. Good at exposing the shit. What about seeing that your vast knowledge of how it should be is what makes the bars of the cage so strong?

It's so simple it's a joke. And one will be fighting with an imaginary "I" like it's a battle. Yeah, listen to Jed more. He is a jerk who embedded his particular unfolding in millions, now they all think they have to stand and fight.

Fight what? Fight WHAT? There is nothing to fight. NOTHING. Seriously.

Nothing to lose, nothing to fight. It's all there already, it always was—everything—thought, feelings, experiences, magic, everything is real. Only the "I" is not. Only the little thought "I" in the head. Look for this thought. It's only a thought. Thought, yes, real. You—no.

No reading, remember?! No FB reading. Feed the chickens. Look at the chickens. Is there any "self" in the chicken? The brain is less developed, a different system, so what? The chicken has no soul but you should? Yes, that's what "YOU" want. How in the world you can have a soul if there is no "you" existing in the first place?!

What is the "chicken" thought pointer? It points to ACTIVITY. The "chicken" in reality is a solid body, a brain, various impulses. Anything personal about this chicken? Unique body/brain activity, yes. Anything else personal, no. What does the thought "I" point to? See what it points to.

Elizabeth: OK, not even Facebook reading... Sorry if I broke the agreement, not an intentional breach of integrity—just being slack and the "vast knowledge" (ha ha!) is not matched by the same degree of focus.

Yes, I agree about Jed McKenna. That one got filtered through some macho thing. Chickens, eh. Yes, I can get that one. An affinity for animals. So, is there any "self" in the chicken? No, only a body, a brain and instinct to survive. Also there is "life" in the chicken. It has an individuality (body, colouring, genetics, behaviour etc.) But does it have a *separate self-controlling life force that belongs just to it*? NO.

It doesn't believe that it controls its life force, its "beingness" and that it can direct its life force (existence, Life, whatever you want to call it). It doesn't hold the thought that it is "Hen X" or that it needs to seek enlightenment from what it already is. It doesn't believe it is ugly or beautiful or needs to have something better than it has (other than for physical survival).

Further up the animal brain-size scale the bigger brains "want" more but it is actually still the same—no belief in a separate, self-controlled, life force ("I") that it owns and that belongs solely to it and is controlled by it. OK, OK... this is coming in closer. This makes a strange sort of sense. I cannot be or have a "piece" of Life, separate and controlled by "me", a belief in my own private piece of Life.

It cannot be "my" life. I cannot break off a piece that is just for me that I direct and control and operate separate from the whole. It is just a misguided belief. An error in seeing... I can stay with this. This is different. "I" points to this belief. A misguided belief in a little broken off piece of Life that is a special "me" that belongs to me and I can direct and control... not possible. Hmm… this is opening something. I am going to follow this. See where it goes.

I see what you say about fighting. I have an image of a little man boxing himself. Mind fighting mind. Just drop it, then? You said "nothing to fight and nothing to lose". OK. I will just put it down.

Chickens, eh! You knew where to get me; ha!

Elena: "Chickens, eh. Yes, I can get that one."

No, you can't. There is no "you" to get it. Investigate this, hard, now. Laser focus. And you cannot stay with this, or not stay with this. There is no "you".

You say—"I am going to follow this."

Oh, yes? You? Really?

Drop the belief that it's hard and needs to be fought. Seriously, look at the chickens some more. Anything really hard for them? Like, do they have to fight to exist? You don't need to fight either. It's "self" fighting to be taken as real.

An actual self is not a part of reality. A chicken does not have to fight to be part of reality—it is. Body, thoughts, feelings—all here. Part of reality. Do you need to fight to observe what's real?

If I give you a cup in your hands and you hold it, it exists, right? So what do you need to do to make the cup stop existing? You need to break it, and it stops existing as a cup, right?

Suppose I extend my hands to you and, lying, say—here is a watermelon.

And I give you an imaginary watermelon.

You take the imaginary watermelon and "hold it". Go ahead, do it. Hold the imaginary watermelon—huge—in between your hands. Now I ask you: what you should do to get rid of this watermelon in your hands?

You can't. There's nothing there. It doesn't make sense to ask that question, and in exactly the same way, it doesn't make sense to ask the question "how can I get rid of the self?" There actually is no self. Never was. Ever. It was always imaginary, right from the start.

Huh. Interesting. But interesting won't free you. Only real investigation into the reality of this will, so investigate.

How do you get rid of the imaginary watermelon in your hands?

How do you get rid of the imaginary self in your head?

Tell me.

Elizabeth: Really, I have not got so many words now. I made a lot of noise before! Not sure how to put this. Don't know quite how it got there, but I was walking out of the bathroom and it hit me, the "lie" of there being an Elizabeth…. Hmm, really can't find the words for it.

Just a certainty that it could be an idea that I had swallowed and never questioned, and even the intellectual understanding of it being a lie was not the same as the impact of *seeing* it for myself. I'll give you some of the back-story that went with this, but it is all words really.

You were right about making a decision. It had been made. It is important, I think, because it is like being open to it. So all the stuff about wanting "me" to exist, all the fighting, it is just the self talking. Just thoughts and concepts. They are not important.

They are happening, but not important... just "noise" and chatter, sidetracks. I am glad you left my questions like "Is there a singularity?" alone. It is just noise, sidetracks. Concepts are endless.

The thoughts circled back to: there is a body, there is a mind. A unique one, but it doesn't possess its own private, personal, separate piece of life. No Elizabeth at the controls.

I am not breathing myself, not growing cells, not digesting food, not emptying the bladder, not living/dying my atoms… I am not "living" myself. There is just "living". Then the words stopped! Without the "ghost in the machine", what I am left with is an existence, just the same as the chickens... being lived (even that is too many words). The thoughts and feelings (and the fighting!) etc. are all the human 'crust' (can't find a word).

Just Life left. It is rather quiet...

Ok—a few more words. I actually *saw* that there was no "I", that it was just something implanted. But I am not sure if it is complete. Was that it? Really? It is so simple just to look!

Elena: You're right on top of it, keep digging, keep investigating, come on!

Elizabeth: Ohhhh... I get it. All the big thoughts I had about enlightenment etc. were getting in the way. All the fancy reading I had done just got sludged up, and slowed down the simple fact of seeing! All that knowledge stuff can find its place (or not) *after* seeing.

Yes. Yes, yes, hey, Elena, this is kind of working itself out! Everything seems so "heavy" with an "I". Without, it is free... shit... it feels... easier... laughing...

... and the self/I is "sticky"... it accumulates stories and anything it can attach to itself? Not sure if this is seeing it, but it feels different... bit crazy right now as I can't sit very still... Have I fallen in an elephant trap here?

Elena: Is there a "you" in reality in any shape or form?

Elizabeth: It seems like there is an "Elizabeth" existence, but without the attachments. I am not sure if this is complete. It feels like an Elizabeth without an "I". Just a stripped-bare existence. Lighter.

Elena, I don't want to be half-cooked. It is just it feels very different. OK... maybe a clearer thing to say is that where I am seeing *from* is different and feels like it will never be the same again.

Elena: No, you are not seeing from anything. There's just seeing—there is no "you". No "you". This is not a joke. This is true. So lighter Elizabeth, or no Elizabeth? Find out which.

Elizabeth: Hello, Elena. OK... keep going... keep looking. I have stopped work for three days up till now and have been on nothing but this. Even my house is looking like a bomb hit it to get at this, but I have kids etc. around all weekend. I am going to keep looking and will post here.

I don't know where to look further, but you have given me enough here to "see". About the watermelon: what do I do to get rid of the imaginary watermelon? Nothing. It doesn't exist.

Elena: You go and take care of your life—and look while you are involved in life. Life is all there is. No need to take yourself out from it. There is nowhere to run from truth. This won't stop being true just because you're busy or distracted. Truth is all there is. So let it continue while you're cleaning your house and do whatever you need to do.

BUT see if you are required for any of it—you—structure Elizabeth. I said it's not hard; when you see it, you will not stop laughing, seriously.

All of it—feelings, sensations, thoughts—is real, yes. The body, movements, everything, everything is real, except Batman, that watermelon I gave you and "I". What do you need to do to get rid of it?

Stop believing in it. It's just a belief. A thought. Break up this "I" and see that it's just a thought. Or prove me wrong.

Elizabeth: Hi, Elena. This may sound odd, but I really do know what I need to see, if that makes sense. Everything you say I understand. It is as if know it but can't bring it in. I know everything you say is true. I understand it. I actually see it in one way. I am not lazy, or stupid or weak.

I can taste it and touch it but not bring it in. But I am not going to let this go. I'll be in touch! And one day I *will* be laughing... Thanks for your time, Elena.

Elena: No, not "one day". NOW. You are at the gate. Do not leave. You can go ahead and take care of stuff, but write to me once a day. Deal?

There is a reason why you don't see or don't know what actually you need to do. There is a reason—that veil that keeps the mind active and holding on to this self. We will break this. No worries.

Just stay with me once a day. It's not linear; you will never figure out this. Never. You need to release the idea that you will ever figure this out. This is not possible to figure out.

This is "you" trying to figure it out. Because there is no "you" in reality, this all becomes like a huge riddle in your head. So just stay with me once a day, whatever it takes. I will not leave. Do not leave.

Elizabeth: OK... no, no chance of me leaving. I wouldn't. I will be in touch once a day. I am away from Monday till Sunday without a computer, though. Thank you, Elena. I appreciate your tenacity!

Elizabeth: Focusing in deep quiet... with everyone here, ironically. Elena, I think this is like a baby being born! I'm not sure. Sitting with it, and what I see is that there is the "Elizabeth-thing" and Life, but no "I" in between. The "I" is a fiction that has hitched a ride.

It all carries on perfectly well without the "I". The "I" thought is just like a parasite that has attached itself. I can taste this, Elena. It is not there yet, but feels so close...

Elizabeth: So, sat with this. It is so fucking frustrating. I see it. Life carries on living me whether I get this or not. I see the "I" thought parasite, but the mind can't let it go. Yes, you are right about the veil. Some kind of protection. I just keep wearing away at it. The watermelon.

Yes, I see it, but the mind is trying to find the concept to erase, and can find no concept, so can't erase it! Bloody, fucking circles! Easier to look at the hen with no independent controller. I look and look. I "see" it but not the way I need to.

Once, a few years ago, I was thinking about "be still and know that I am God" (not the Christian god). And for a while I completely let go and saw that only life was running the show, that there was no "I". What the fuck is this about? I can see it, understand it, taste it, but the mind won't let go. Sorry to vent here...

Elena: Do not wait for anything special. That moment of letting go and seeing only the life running the show was a state, a transient state; it showed you the truth. Now we are here to make the mind realise it. Does a baby in a crib have an "I"? What does the baby see/feel?

Does the baby feel separate from the flow? Did you feel separate from the flow at that moment? You saw it—no separation. The mind creates this separation to operate in the world. To see that "I" does not exist is nothing more than to realise that life is running the show.

Would anything change viscerally? Not necessarily. Life was before you saw it, and is the same life after. No angels will come down. Nope, the same body, the same feelings, the same shit will remain. Like when you actually understood that Santa does not exist, did anything change?

Maybe sad feelings came and went. But the point is that after that you never took Santa at face value. You relaxed and went with the "Santa show" for years to come. You never had that "seeking Santa's presents under the tree" uneasy feeling again: "what if am not good enough and he won't bring me presents this year?" Because there was a knowledge of truth.

Same here. Look at the "I" thought more: how it comes and grabs everything that's happening.

Elizabeth: OK, Elena, that is really clear and I will take some time with it. Actually, some time out and about today showed me, interestingly, that the clarity from understanding, even as much as the last few days have revealed, has stopped the seeking and hunting for the answer.

It is clear to me, even if the separation still exists. There is nothing more to do really except follow your suggestions. No more books to read, no more teachers to listen to. I feel a resolution of years and years of seeking. The reality of this is clear and that, for now, is good. The "I" feels as if it is fading.

Elena: It doesn't NEED to FADE. It's not about identity FADING.

It's about the truth, Elizabeth—that identity doesn't point to anything. Fade, not fade—whatever. The point is that it is FICTION. The strength of the fiction is irrelevant—the FACT that it IS fiction is KEY.

Look at the "I" thought. That's all is needed. Look behind the "I" thought. What's there?

Elizabeth: I tried some gentle speculation. What if I accept that there may have been a monumental lie given to me from birth that there was an "I", and this was totally accepted and reinforced by everything around me. What would it mean if there were no me/I?

What if it was all a lie? The difference with looking this time was that I relaxed and allowed the mind to play with it rather than trying to force it to accept. I felt a strange spacey-ness, then a spaciousness opened, an expansion into everything.

It seemed that the "I" was something that wanted to grab everything, make everything belong to it, attach to everything, and then spin stories. What was left? An existence that was everything, and the I-entity (of thoughts, like a parasite). This is how I sat for an hour or so, wondering what was happening.

Elena: Yes, nice—now get back to looking. Focus.

There is no "you". Is this true?

Elizabeth: No, there is no me. Behind the "I" is just a great emptiness...

Elena: Is there a "you" that is living life? What drives life?

Elizabeth: OK, plain looking at reality. "Is there a 'you' that is living life?" No, not a "me" living life. There is a life living itself, a physical existence. Nothing "underneath" it, no "controller" I. What drives life? I don't know. It just arises, patterns within patterns.

Elena: You can now release looking for something that you saw does not exist. You can just go ahead and live. Simply. You know, chop wood, carry water? Yep, do that. Can you do that?

Stop striving. That's it. Just that reality, the truth of it. See how deep it goes?

Elizabeth: Yes! I didn't realise it was so practical and simple. It makes me laugh! Driving back there was just the brain and the body driving—no "me" there. How on earth would a "me" drive a car? Funny.

An imaginary "I" at the steering wheel. Just read something about "peeing"... ha ha... no "self" to do the peeing. Ahhhh....

Elena: Hahaha! Great! Have a great trip! Much love.

Elizabeth: Thanks, Elena. And for the patience!

Elena: Good work. Strong, determined. I wish I could hug you!

And it's not fancy at all. It's so simple. So the root was seeing. Now all remaining shit will start to be shed from the system as unnecessary. A life based on inspiration and without fear is the best life a human can live. Enjoy the unfolding!

Elizabeth: The urgency to show others makes sense now. Thank you soooo much! Elizabeth

Christie

When Christie came to me she was in a bad way. She had been suffering deeply and really needed help. First we worked through the heavy feelings, and once the suffering lifted, she started to look. It took some time to see and more time to settle. It was heart-warming for me to witness this transformation from somebody completely broken to somebody who now can enjoy life. I'm really happy for Christie.—I. C.

Christie: I'll try and give you the Readers Digest version:

I'm in the midst of an enormous 'life' drama. I'm fifty years old and last April my husband and I started reading Jed McKenna. We had been following this "train" for years, but he really brought it home for us.

Then, out of nowhere, the husband tells me he has to go into this "dark place" alone and needs me to move on—to move out. So I'm trying to make sense of this drama. The movers just delivered my stuff this morning so I have lots of time to think while I try and rebuild, well, everything.

Darren tells me you're the one to talk to. Can you guide me through this?

Ilona: Oh, wow, that's really horrible, I'm so sorry to hear what's happened with you.

Thank you so much for writing. It is my pleasure to assist and help you through seeing the illusion.

I read Jed's books and it brought a lot of darkness. I was doing his 'spiritual autolysis' thing and sometimes it felt horrible.

The good thing about Jed is that he was one of the first to bring a very stripped-down, no-nonsense attitude to all this stuff. The bad thing is that there's a very strong undercurrent of darkness and nihilism to his work, and it really can suck a person down.

There is no need for that. We can look at the centre of illusion, knock down the core, take out the root and the rest will unfold naturally.

So I will be asking you some questions and all you need to do is answer them with 100% honesty about what feels true.

Deal?

So let's look at where you are at the moment. There is no separate self at all in real life. Is this true?

Christie: Thank you.

I believe that is true, and see it with clarity at times, but 50% of the time I find myself sucked into the drama of the shock and heartbreak of my situation.

Making it "stick" seems impossible when I'm still feeling like I have to think about and control the basics—roof over head, food in the cabinets, money, change of address card, unpacking. A thousand little things that have to be done and I try to surrender with the understanding that it will, in fact, get done.

I will give you 100% honesty and am excited about a process which does not involve autolysis—I tried that for a month before this turn of events and didn't feel I was getting anywhere.

Ilona: Great! Let's start! So... from now on please answer with what you see, not what you believe. We need to go past belief and test everything.

OK, so tell me, when you look at "there is no self at all in real life", what happens inside? Is there fear, resistance, unease, doubt? Can you identify the feeling?

Christie: I recognise a little unease/fear, but also some relief. During the times when I can really see it clearly, all I feel is relief. Like the pressure is off and it almost feels like joy. But I can't stay there.

Ilona: The next thing we look at is resistance itself. As there are many beliefs in the system, some of them conflict and fight with each other. Resistance rises as a result of conflict inside.

You can feel it in the body and it's an unpleasant feeling. There is a little fear involved sometimes, and we'll work through that if it comes up.

The thing about fear is this—if there is truly no self at all, then there's nothing to protect, right? Only illusion.

The body is real—so protecting that is fair enough. The mind is real, so again, fair enough. But the thing that owns the body and the mind? There's nothing there. So you don't need to be afraid of protecting the self—there is no self to protect.

Can you look at the possibility that there is no self at all again? Notice the fear. Identify it and ask it to come closer, just observe it. Don't go into the detail of the fear, but look at it as a phenomenon in itself. You can ask it to reveal its wisdom. Just stay with it for a little while and see what happens.

You can close your eyes and let that fear be there, sit with it, look at how perfectly it guards something. Honour it. It sounds strange, but do it.

Then look: what is behind the fear? Is there anything at all? What do you find?

Christie: It's funny that you mention that fear. I've been thinking about that part a lot lately.

To be perfectly honest, I've toyed with the idea of suicide quite a bit these past few weeks, even written letters to my loved ones asking for their forgiveness (won't be sending them), but pray for death daily.

So I have wondered about this fear and where it comes from since I sincerely hope to die. I'll think on this for a little while and let you know what I'm able to come up with. Thank you.

Ilona: You don't need to die. What "dies" is illusion. It may feel like the end of the world, but it's only the end for the imaginary self. The tooth fairy is not real either, and when you found that out, the tooth fairy did not die, no matter what Peter Pan says.

Don't give up. Ok? Don't ever give up. Sometimes life is hard, but it can always be simple. You can do this.

Facing fear itself is not going to kill you, it's just going to reveal what fear is, not so much the content as the mechanism itself.

We don't have to be scared of fear. Fear is here to protect. It feels dark and solid. But it's only fear. As they say, False Evidence Appearing Real.

Just bring it closer and look behind, you will be surprised.

Much much love.

Christie: I've spent some time with that fear and looked at it closely. What I find is that it's not a fear of "death" at all but a fear of meaninglessness. That what I have seen as "my life" may have no value, purpose, has been for nothing. That the special and unique "me" never was. And that creates the physical and emotional feeling of fear. When I look closer, I don't see. Is this ego?

P.S. I've wondered about the character Julie from Jed's first book and about the scene at the cafe when they meet after she's gone through the process. She had to leave, crying, before she could come back and sit down. I know it's fiction but this never made sense to me. If she was truly "gone" why was she crying?

Ilona: I don't remember the scene very well as I read it a year ago. Let's leave it for a bit and we can come back to it later.

Meaninglessness. Look—it's not life that's the illusion. It's self. Sometimes life has meaning, sometimes not, but the self never has, because it is not real. Life just is. Now, with that said, the mind is always looking for meaning and creating it—often just to feed this illusion of self.

This kind of meaning—selfish meaning—is very destructive and divisive. Selfless meaning is the only meaning that's real, and that can't ever go away. If anything, this will bring you closer to it.

But what is the meaning of a flower? Does it need to have a meaning to exist? Every flower is unique; even if you have blossoms on the same branch, they are each individual and unique. That uniqueness does not disappear.

Oh, and uh—Ego does not exist. It's a story.

What is here is life going on plus labelling by the mind. Which is also going on by itself. The illusion is that it is "me" thinking.

But "me" does not exist in reality.

Can you look here now and tell me if it's true?

Christie: I can say that is true. I see the truth of it more every day. The process seems to have a life of its own and "I'm" just watching it unfold. But it's two steps forward and one step back.

I've enjoyed reading your blog with the tips and other people's experiences. I began writing in a journal back in April, but haven't in the last several weeks. This process is painful for me, or maybe it's my life circumstances. I've begun to wonder if all this is happening for the reason of awakening.

Is there a "Grand Design" or a single intelligence behind life's living?

I have another question: I can see that life is living itself and "I" is an illusion, but whenever I think about the suffering that my husband has caused me, I can't seem to fit that in with the "everything is as it should be" model. I feel angry and hurt and it pulls me back into "me".

Ilona: Yes, Christie, life is living itself. But no—sometimes life is very nasty, and unfair, and unnecessary suffering happens. The point is not that if you believe really, really strongly that everything's ok, it will be. That's magical thinking; children do that.

The point is that, in real life, it's not happening to anyone. It's just happening. And if you see that, and the flow of what's happening, you can move through the bad things better, with clarity and freedom. And, in real life, resolve those situations in a better way.

OK, next step, we examine thoughts. Can you close your eyes after reading this and find in there something that always is present? That sense of beingness. "Am".

Notice the space, notice thoughts appearing and disappearing. Where do they come from? Can you control them? Can you stop a thought in middle? Can you see how every event in awareness, be it sensation, sound or feeling, is labelled by the mind?

The mind is a labelling machine. It immediately translates what's going on into words. Plus, when nothing is going on, the mind goes into the past and future and chats constantly.

Can you get back to me with what you find?

Christie: I can sense the beingness. I've noticed the thoughts and wonder if these thoughts come from the same place as in a deer deciding which direction to walk, or a bird making "decisions" about what step to take, where to fly. Are our thoughts from the same One? Only more complicated?

I see how this mind labels and categorises. I've wondered about how past and future are constantly a part of the inner narration. Are we all insane, as Tolle says?

I've been up all night. I don't know how much longer I can keep this up. I need some relief, to stop thinking about it or to find just an ounce of joy somewhere. My mind and body feel so weak and broken down. Thank you for being here.

Ilona: Christie, you're going through a lot. Be gentle with yourself.

Now let's come back to it. Thoughts come and go from nothing. Void if you like. "I" is also just a thought. It has no power, no control, it cannot think. It's just a thought like "deer", or "tree", or whatever.

When you look at thoughts, notice that some thoughts refer to something that is real—"tree", "table", "window", "hand".

But not all thoughts refer to real things. Look at the thought "I". Is there an "I" in the room? Can you see that "I" is just a label referring to thoughts about "I", nothing else? And it appears and disappears effortlessly. It has no control at all.

Can you see that?

I'm here for you; we will work this out. There's not much left.

Seeing is happening already, without a seer. All is just flowing effortlessly. Can you notice that?

There is no you to notice it either, just noticing. Happening. "I notice" is just a label for experience.

Write what is being seen in the room at the moment.

Christie: What is being seen in the room at the moment: lots of boxes that need unpacking and miscellaneous chaos. Quiet. Intense emptiness. And this body typing on the iPad.

Ilona: Nice. I'd love an iPad.

How is the typing process going? Look there, what happens there? In detail, please.

Christie: Thought arises and fingers type. I watched the video you had posted on your site and was amazed about the six seconds that it takes for the brain to inform the mind. All very confusing in this context.

I feel like a puppet, acting on thought that is not mine. I read one time about the artist, author or songwriter being nothing but like a limb of the One. You can't be prideful of a hand that paints a nice picture or a pen that writes a good story.

Is this right?

Ilona: Yes, it's right. I came to see that I'm not an artist, just a brush. How can a brush be proud? There is no one to be proud.

There is no you to feel as a puppet. Of course thought is not yours, there is no you at all to own anything.

So look: thought arises, fingers type, all this is happening by itself. How can there be a director?

There is no you to see through. It's just looking through happening by itself. The brain is resolving the conflict by itself.

What is being noticed?

Christie: I think I'm there—only there is something that wants to hold on. Maybe fear of relinquishing control. But I'm beginning to sense that there was never any control by "me" to begin with. More time, I think.

Ilona: Great!

Seeing is happening! The feeling of holding on is happening, but there is no you to hold on, just a feeling arising and labelling happening.

No, there never was any control by "you", like there never was a Santa!

What's happening?

Christie: Hoping that there would be some relief with seeing. No "me" but still much pain. How can this be? How can this suffering continue? How can this Christie continue life?

Ilona: Tell me, please, what is Christie?

Christie: Nothing. A paintbrush. A costume. An expression of a thought. No more than a tree or a stone. That's why there's no understanding of why it continues to cry. Shouldn't there be some disconnection from this emotion?

Ilona: Look from a slightly different angle: there is a story playing out, a story, where Christie is the main character. Can you see her? Can you see how beautiful she is? Can you appreciate Christie? I appreciate Christie very much.

There is no driver, but there is the story, a real story. Real fiction. Christie is here now. Look.

The suffering is part of the story. As stories go, you never know what's round the corner.

Who is suffering? Is there a sufferer?

Christie: Thank you for your help and your kindness. You are a lovely expression.

Ilona: How is the world looking today?

Christie: Much better. Much.

Ilona: Could you answer me these questions, so I know precisely where you are:

1) Is there a "you", at all, anywhere, in any way, shape or form?
2) Explain in detail what the self is and how it works.
3) How does it feel to be liberated?

Thank you.

Christie: I don't know anything right now. There's too much in my head. Just dealing with the details and drama of what's going on in this life is overwhelming.

I made an appointment with a therapist for this afternoon to help me with the emotional mess. I won't be mentioning the "no self" business to him, but I'm on the verge of losing my sanity.

Thanks for staying with me. I'll keep in touch.

Ilona: Let whatever comes up be OK...

Just watch it pass by. Nothing is here to stay, all impermanent... The overwhelming feelings are not permanent, this too shall pass.

It is a huge shock to the belief system, yes, and all beliefs that have nowhere to attach to are starting to fall. Hold on to nothing. Holding on only creates suffering. Let it all melt away. Release even holding on to your sanity. It's all just a concept. These are just thoughts passing by. There is no "I" to be sane or insane.

Good that you are seeing a therapist. He may help you to calm down... Please keep me updated. Let me know if I can help you with anything at all.

Lots of love.

Christie: Thank you so much for this—"let whatever comes up be OK". "Holding on only creates suffering". "Release." The very words I needed to hear. I am releasing. I've read this e-mail six times. I should be seeing you once a week. You are such a gift.

Ilona: After you done, you won't have to see anyone.

How was your therapist yesterday?

Let's give it some time to settle and we carry on. Write to me when you are ready.

Christie: Ilona, I think the train wreck portion of the program is over.

The seeing is happening and the "me" is disappearing (has disappeared? Was never there?). The suffering I was (am) going through feels more and more like just suffering, but not of a "me". All day today I "saw" it, recognised IT. It's hard to explain, but a definite shift has occurred. I was awareness for the majority of the day. But I've thought of a couple of questions:

When you are involved in an experience, and your mind is on whatever is happening, brain work you could say, is there some part of "you" that forgets that you don't exist? Or do you always "think" about not being?

Another question: When I switch the channel on the radio without thinking and it surprises me because I had not thought to do it, who is surprised? Here's where I feel I am today:

#1. "Is there a 'you'?" There doesn't appear to be a "me". I am curious how you will answer my question about who was surprised by the radio—my sense is that the answer is the mind which thinks that it's the thinker—that mind still operates as if it exists, but it isn't real. I don't have this completely understood yet.

#2. "Explain in detail what the self is and how it works." See #1. I can regurgitate what I've read, but I need to take some time to spell it out clearly in my own words...

#3. "How does it feel to be liberated?" Today, it has felt free, unburdened by worry of making wrong choices. I've kept your words close today. Surrender.

More later.

Ilona: I'm sooo glad to hear, Christie, that the shift has occurred and suffering is dropping. One more step—awareness just is. There is no you in there, it is not personal. Look at a cat, is he awareness? It's just like a space which notices itself. Tell me, does awareness need an "I" to be aware?

As for the first question: Until all old programming is cleared and processed, the mind refers to "no you". Then it just drops. You'll see, it's not something I can explain. I don't think now about it at all, just living life. It may take a few months to clean the clutter.

Second: yes, who was surprised? Was it just a feeling of surprise appearing? And mind labelled it as "I'm surprised?"

Think from that perspective, really get inside it, then answer all three questions again.

Much love!

Christie: When you went through this, did you have nightmares? I have horrible nightmares EVERY night. I don't even like walking into the bedroom anymore.

Ilona: No, I did not have nightmares, no, but it's different for everyone. As I said, you're going through a lot, I think many in your position would have nightmares too. They're just nightmares, they'll pass.

Christie: To be honest, I've spent much of the weekend trying to distract myself from the heaviness of this no self business.

But this evening I've been drawn to Eckhart Tolle. I have some of his books on audio and I find his voice to be very soothing. I'm taking his advice and spending time facing and embracing my grief, saying yes to what is and coming to terms with the fact that no one has any choice in what they do.

I have looked long and hard and can find no evidence of a "me". I feel Source acting through me and believe that all "I" need to do is allow it without resistance. Surrender is difficult to maintain. I can surrender fifty times a day and find that I need to surrender again. It's like I've always heard of forgiveness—it's not a one-time thing, it has to be done over and over.

Ilona: I see that there is still a lot inside that needs to be released. Of course, so many years of piling it up and stuffing feelings as far away as possible. One thing: notice that surrender is also happening by itself, no matter what thoughts about it say.

Yes it's a ride without driver. Any time you feel like you are driving, it's just another idea ready to be released.

It will get lighter and clearer in time. Relax more, deeper. All is taken care of.

So maybe you are ready to review the last three questions again?

Much love.

Christie: OK, here are my answers today:

Is there a me? There is a body which functions on its own like any animal. The "me" which was there was an illusion created by the ego.

What the self is and how it works—the self is the mistaken attempt by the ego to project itself as separate from everything else. I AM the source of everything that is, acting and experiencing everything as and through this form of Christie. Christie is limited to her experiences just as a dog or cat can only experience through its own being. But they are only tools used to experience and to act out the One Life that lives through everything. I AM that. The self is no thing.

How does it feel to be liberated? I would like to say it feels peaceful and easy, but the experience of this life continues, at times, to be unbearable. Knowing that I AM in this form may take some more time, but I experience a constant drive to end this life. I understand that the thoughts are of The Source so "I" am torn as to act on these thoughts or to simply watch them pass and continue on to tomorrow.

I realise after reading this that Christie sounds like a terrible mess, but that's just a label, too.

Ilona: Thank you, Christie. Two things that seem odd: illusion was created by the ego. Is the ego real? Can it create anything?

"I AM the source of everything that is." What would happen to everything that is if there was no you? Can you look a bit deeper here? What is the source?

It's all unravelling already. The mess is getting cleared up.

With love.

Christie: Illusion must then be created as everything else is created—by the One Source. The nature of this "life". You're right; it doesn't make sense that the ego, which is not real, could create anything. Is this true?

By "I am the source" I mean that I am not "me", in this body, this individual, but rather a part of the One Source. Call it God or Life or It. I read somewhere that sunlight flowing through a red glass appears red, through green glass, green. It appears through this being as "me", but I am still a part of that 'sun'. If there was no "me", nothing would change. I see it as the realisation of the 'I AM'.

Am I on the right track?

Ilona: Perfectly.

God = life = reality = 1

Self = me = I = zero.

Once this is seen, then everything falls into place. Seems that you have graduated!

Is there anything else I can help you with?

We have a free and open group for all new "liberated", a place to share, explore, support when needed. If you don't have an account, you may create one, doesn't even need to be in your own name if you don't want it to be. Would be great if you joined. Just find me through my blog.

Much love.

Christie: There's still some unresolved garbage, but I really appreciate your help. Thanks for the invitation; I'll look for a link on your blog page. I don't mind if you put this on your page, but I would rather you change my name since [redacted] is my real name.

I'll look for you on Facebook and hope to talk to you again soon. It's been such a gift having you to communicate with.

Much Love.

Ilona: Thank you.

It's been a pleasure to assist. Any time you have a question; I'm just an e-mail away. But from now on life is going to get interesting. All is working out. For me in the beginning it felt like everything started to fall into place, all unravelling in perfect ways.

••◆••

Some time later I received the following message from Christie—I. C.

Christie: It had been about four months since I started reading Jed McKenna's books, and the idea of no self was on my mind all the time. I started writing, trying to peel myself apart to get down to where there was nothing, but there was always something, and the mind chewed on it and turned it around and tried to make it fit.

I bought books by other authors and was always trying to find a way to get my head around it and make it stick. It was all intellect, the mind trying to figure it out. It wasn't until life was turned completely upside down that there was an opening.

The identity was clinging so hard to the heartache and misery, "my story", but it was that VERY suffering that I first was able to recognise as suffering—appearing without the "me".

Over time, with your help, I looked, really spent time alone with what I Am. Then I began to see the emotions passing through and relaxed the grip of the "I". There was no sudden "happening" as I had anticipated; it felt as if the bulk of "me" just dissipated like a ghost. I say the bulk because I've found, just over the past week or two, that the mind slips "me" in every now and then. It's like the mind keeps trying to recreate a "me". But there never was one.

Life lives directly, experiences directly and continues the "story" by itself. There is recognition when the mind does this and then it falls away. I "see" Life acting through others and recognise it as such, but still feel annoyed, frustrated or angry or sad at times. But there is no "me" to claim it! Only seeing, feeling, experiencing these emotions—watching them pass through.

One other thing worth noting: This person I've claimed as "me" has been physically very tense for many years with the burden of imagined control (and perhaps guilt of past mistakes, etc.)

Have seen pain specialists about it over years. These are noticeably better. Physically, there is a relaxation of muscles in the neck and back which have caused this pain in the past.

Ever Grateful for your pointing.

Richard

This man was confirmed by his Theravada meditation teacher to have attained Stream Entry (a classical Buddhist attainment station). I asked him to explain the experience, and then we went ahead with looking into the nature of reality. At the end he proclaimed that our work led him to the reality of actual "Stream Entry", when the illusion of "I" was actually seen through.—E. N.

Richard: Hey, Elena.

I have been following the direct pointing thread on the DhO site, and would like to follow up on your invitation for pursuing the realisation of no-self. I spent a great deal of time on Saturday and Sunday reflecting on and contemplating. At one point there was a clear "aha!" moment. I went through the exercise of looking at objects and recognised each one of them as real.

The table is real. The computer is real. The leg is real. The hand is real. The self is... gasp ... nowhere to be found...

Elena: Great.

Richard: There was a sense of exhilaration.

Elena: Yes.

Richard: As well as great relief.

Elena: Yes.

Richard: The next morning, I woke up feeling slightly changed; lighter.

Elena: Yes.

Richard: Less sticky.

Elena: Yes.

Richard: There was a clear "feeling" of non-self as opposed to an "understanding" that there is no self.

Elena: Yes.

Richard: That being said, the effect has worn off quickly. The insight lasts as long as many of the other insights into how my mind works, so I am wondering:

a) Whether that was the experience of non-self you are referring to?

Elena: It may be, we can continue to chat and see.

Richard: b) If it was, how can my direct experience be deepened and sustained?

Elena: Liberation is very simple. It is not sustaining some belief or experience. It is simply seeing the truth of the illusion, and then letting it unfold in the order of your own body/mind makeup.

The only thing that's gone is the belief that there is a "me" entity/structure. That structure was binding all the beliefs, tensions and thoughts about oneself together. As it is seen through, this mess of stuff that was built on that assumption will start to gradually fall away.

Seeing that there is no "you" is not an end, just a beginning. BUT, without it, all the effort was coming from the self itself in order to maintain it. Even years in meditation can serve to maintain a "spiritual", "hardcore", "dharmic" self.

So I ask you now: look and tell me if there is a "you" in any shape or form in reality.

Richard: Very little. The thing that decides, the thing that has an intent, that generates the intent; but I am doubting it now, the intent seems to come from nowhere and then disappears. In fact, I only recognise the intent after the fact (i.e. "I must have decided to type" because I am typing now).

But also, when I make a conscious decision that I will type now, I don't know where that decision came from. I can only conclude that I must have decided it. Only now I am doubting that I did.

In interest of full disclosure, I should mention that I have also been an insight practitioner and have attained stream entry, confirmed by a teacher in August of last year. So my starting point for this experiment was probably farther along then most people you normally work with.

Elena: Tell me what was confirmed by your teacher. In simple language, how you would explain it to someone with no spiritual background?

Richard: I reported to the teacher that, when closing my eyes, I felt that my mind and body were made of mist. I experienced waves of exhilaration, followed by a sense of constriction, followed by relief, followed by a discontinuity in consciousness. The discontinuity was subtle, for lack of a better term it felt like a subtle "blink".

Since then, the dharma has been doing its thing. I have had more dramatic discontinuities, but the permanent change seems to be that there is simply a lot more space between thoughts. Oftentimes, the mind literally feels like a car idling at the stop light, where in the past it was always in one gear or another.

Elena: There is no "you" to make conscious decisions. It just seems so because the thought came that there is a "you", then the thought came that you will make a decision, then the thought came describing the decision.

Impulses to the body. Typing happening. Thought. Thought. Thought. Typing.

Where is "you"?

Thought exists. The body exists. You do not.

"I don't know where that decision came from. I can only conclude that I must have decided it. Only now I am doubting that I did. "

Good. Look deeper and tell me more.

About your "Stream Entry" realisation. If they call it stream entry, that's fine, but I would say that stream entry is this—when one sees through the illusion of a self living life, one also sees the unity of life itself.

Cultivating that sense of the united flow of things—that I would call 'stream entry'.

Anything before that—including very high states—it's all operating in the field of the self. I had what you described eight or nine years ago. Exactly what you described—mind/body dissolution—bang. When I came back, self grabbed that experience and made it "very deep self".

I don't want to downplay the experience. It is indeed very transformational—it's cleared the mind so much. It took me eight years after that state. It took you much less.

Continue to look.

Look at this:

It rains.

Is there anything raining rain? It rains.

But then of course, you could say—the clouds. But what's clouding? The sky? What's skying? The earth? What's earthing?

What's living life?

Is there anything living life?

All different patterning of the same thing—Existence existing.

Look deeper.

Look now.

Look around.

Tell me what's going on in your head now.

Richard: OK, so a self is just is a thought, I accept that. But it it's a thought that keeps arising. I guess the point is that this is not a problem as long as it's viscerally clear that the thought of a self is just that—a thought, nothing more.

I started thinking about death. I was going to say that when we die we become a noun, but that's not true, because the second we stop breathing we start decaying. So, yeah, everything is a process, a verb. This led to thoughts about birth; since we are a process, it's not quite clear when we were born. But I think I am digressing.

The theme of death is not a coincidental, though. There are flashes, moments when there is a strange sense that everything is haunted. It's there in form but somehow lifeless, in the same way a ghost town is physically real but at the same time it is an eerie reminder of what was once a town.

Elena: Yes. I just do not like here the word "accept". It's not about accepting this, like you tick a box and agree. Please, please, do not accept anything—look and see for yourself.

So, let's refocus. When you drive or walk etc. there is no driver.

Just as there is no breather. Breathing is just happening.

Is this true?

Richard: Yes, driving, walking, breathing: they all just happen, the second I notice them, they are claimed as "I\me" doing the breathing. It's a reflex. It's automatic. I was going to say there's not much I can do about it, but then realised there is no "I" to do anything about it.

What about getting lost in thought? I was going to say, who is doing the thinking, who is lost? But, again, thinking and "losting" just happen.

I am not convinced, though, that saying that things just happen is the same as saying there is no self, because a sense of self is more of a "feeling" than a thought. The feeling is there every time I notice that things just happen.

Just to be clear, I am not saying that there is a self or there that there isn't one (because the thought/feeling is clearly there), just that my recognition that things "just happen" is not the same is what I mean by "there is seeing but no seer, thinking but no thinker".

Elena: What you are talking about is a state, a unity state, or whatever you choose to call it. The state is not permanent. It can come, but it's impossible to hold it.

You can cultivate the flow—that's true. And it's only possible to do that in a sustainable way once you've seen through the illusion that the flow is broken by the self.

It gives an insight into the nature of being. There are two, maybe more, but I will say for the sake of this endeavour, two possibilities after the state is gone. One—the self comes back with even more conviction and grabs that experience and colours itself in more "specialness", more "spirituality".

And another possibility is what we are after here: when you saw that, yes, there is only seeing, thinking, no "me" structure in all these movement of life, it's just an illusion. You come back and KNOW this. No need to remember it every moment. Realising the illusion of the self is very simple—just that—realising that self is an illusion.

Basically, nothing will change overnight, BUT at the same time, now all life will be springing from this fundamental knowing of the truth. And it will all be unfolding from that, gradually unrolling through every inch of the body/mind system. This is what is called stream entry. The beginning of the end.

Write more to me, just blabber, so I can see where we stand. Focus on seeing, on looking at what is. Take something in your life that's happening now, like moving and walking, and write anything that comes up.

Richard: As people walked by, the thought came to me: those poor guys there not free.

Elena: Yes, lots of people around to help. But also keep in mind: it's not these 'selves' that we need to help—there are no selves to help. It's just life, all the different forms and processes. It's all movement of consciousness, and if consciousness wakes up in one embodiment, the ripples go all over and wake up other embodiments without even explicit guiding and looking.

Some may feel like a brick is coming down on them, when they never even searched for anything.

Richard: How silly of me. I am not free.

Elena: And you never will be, because there is no "I" to free. But freedom can happen—just see that truth.

Richard: Still a clear sense that things are happening; reaching for the drink, cutting food, keep telling my self there is no need for a "me".

Elena: Good. And you don't need to tell yourself this. You just know this, no reminder necessary. Once seen, never unseen. It may seem like when you sit in a movie theatre and get taken over by the scene, but then you know a moment later that you are in a movie theatre and that this scene is just an illusion.

But imagine somebody whose life is in the chair of the movie theatre, constantly watching movies. He is living as if it was his reality and all this was real. You need to drag this man outside and point to him that what he was seeing there is an illusion. When he sees it just once, even if he returns to his seat, he will know. He may forget sometimes, but never again will he take the movie to be reality.

Richard: Today was a tough day. This morning it occurred to me that I (or the mind/body process) was going through the classical insight stages. The heightened awareness, the religious "zeal", the anxiety, the fear, the sense of wanting it all to end, they are all classical insight stages.

This realisation was helpful in that it pointed to the fact that the Self is there resisting/identifying with the experiences, once I saw that the unpleasant experiences had subsided (in insight lingo that would be early equanimity stage).

Elena: Remember, you are facing a really tricky one—self—that can play all kind of tricks. You can't cut your own hair. Same here. Write to me. Write as it happens, not next day with all your conclusions.

But listen—if you gauge freedom by whether the mind is attaching labels of self to things, you're missing the point.

It's not about stopping those labels—it's about seeing that they're not stuck TO anything. They're just labels, hovering there, like all fiction, like any fictional character, Harry Potter, Jane Eyre, Xena the Warrior Princess. Just labels, that don't actually refer to something in reality.

Richard: Right now, I can't point to a self, but I don't feel like reality is just happening. There is still a sense of me controlling things,

Elena: Look into this sense of self. What is it? Break it into components.

Richard: For example, I was going through dark stages of insight, recognised them and used familiar techniques to move beyond them.

Elena: Hmm. Didn't we talk about this work in the beginning? I ask a question. You go look, then come back and give me the most honest answer. Didn't we talk about it? Did I say anything about going back and doing your familiar thing/technique?

Richard: I don't feel like any of that just happened. There was recognising, investigating, relaxing, accepting... but I still claim those as something that a "me/I" observed/initiated/controlled. At the same time, there is doubt whether there was any "me/I" there at all.

Elena: Look at the doubt. Doubt is a feeling arising, just a feeling. You don't need to analyse why it is there. Invite doubt closer; it's here anyway. And ask doubt what it wants to reveal to you; what information it's brought. Then you just casually sit, shut up and listen.

Same with fear. You did some technique yesterday, maybe meditated or whatever you did, you just petted the fear and it went away.

Next time you have fear, if you do, write to me. You need to stare fear in the eye. No more equanimity techniques for now. You have to promise me. You can do whatever you want later on, after. Now—naked honesty; clear, precise writing of whatever comes up.

You have your ideas about liberation. It being this dropping of identification.

It is NOT the dropping of identification. That's impossible, because the mind just churns out these labels, as part of its structure. It's seeing that all this identification is fundamentally fictional, because there was no you, is no you, and never will be a you in real life.

You need to drop that expectation, it's a caricature of what this is. Drop it now. Drop it. Seriously. Write to me what you know about liberation with complete honesty, without referencing what you've read and what you've heard. Just what you know for sure.

Go.

Richard: I want to say nothing because my mind just goes blank when I try to express what I know, but to me it's a shift in perception. I experience it quite often, something where I feel transparent like Teflon. Nothing sticks, like I have nothing to hold on to.

When I look at people, it's as if there is nothing there. Just their body, their form. It's liberating yet scary at the same time. I felt quite a bit of that yesterday. I was literally feeling nauseated, in the same way you can get on a roller coaster.

Obviously, the nausea and the fear are not liberation, maybe not even the transparent/Teflon quality of experience, but it's in that neighbourhood; being able to abide peacefully and continuously in that experience is liberation.

I just want to make sure we are on the same page here: I didn't pacify the fear/anxiety, I recognised that the fear/anxiety is not me and stopped resisting it. Is that different from staring it in the eye?

Elena: OK, fine, let's believe it for now.

"Being able to abide peacefully and continuously in that experience is liberation."

It's called being dead.

Look at that "constant reflex". Look closer. What it is. It's thought. Is this true?

Richard: I tried and tried, and eventually I realised I am looking for something that isn't there. Then I asked what was there, and what I saw/felt were peaceful sensations.

I sank into that a bit, and the contrast between the tension and struggle and the peace I felt was striking. Then a phone call came in that I had to take. One hour later, I tried to locate the self and there was less of a reflex, or I should say there was less of a struggle.

Elena: No control, yes. But what you do, what you do... watch out for escaping into familiar territory. You build up this really thick dharma self, a really clever, deep, wise one. I want you to direct your attention and look at it. Honestly. Now write what comes up in your head about it.

Write and we'll look at any doubts one by one.

Richard: One doubt I have is whether I am agreeing that there is no "me" because it's too difficult to find it. As I write this, I realise how silly that is—the "me" feels so real, it should be easy to find. Then another doubt arises: well, you can't find it because the thing doing the looking is you. How can you see yourself without a mirror? I don't have a good response for that, do you?

Elena: Release the struggle. What you are looking for is not there, you're right, otherwise you would find it very easily. DO you struggle a lot to find the computer or your hand or a thought?

You don't struggle because computers, hands and thoughts exist. They are part of reality. Self is not part of reality. Self is part of reality the same way Batman is now in your room. Try to see Batman. Can you see him? You can easily access a thought of Batman, yes—thoughts exist, a bunch of thoughts—and you have an image of Batman. But other than that? Is he real? Can you shoot up a bat signal, and call him to fight the real Joker? No. Illusion. Fiction.

The self is the same thing. The harder you try to see it, the more you see its futility. You can't see something that does not exist, you're right.

So when you are in your daily life and you feel like self exists, what's changed? Has self miraculously become existent? No. You're just being too lazy to see what it actually is. So look, don't make me start cursing, OK?

You feel like you are a self sitting here. Look what is there: sensations, thought, feeling, whatever; break it down.

Do it. Look. Seriously, look. Do not take even 5% of your focus to analyse it and compare it to your dharmic knowledge of enlightenment. Just fkn look. That is the only thing you need to do now. Like you are a six-year old boy.

You've never heard the signs of classical enlightenment bullshit, never heard what all these signs that you disperse your focus on means. Drop it. Drop it. Drop it.

Otherwise you will be sitting in meditation and searching for years to come. Drop all this useless "dharma knowledge". Really. It's just this massive weight around your neck, weighing you down with these ridiculous, cartoon expectations.

100% focus on LOOKING at what is really there and what is not. That's it.

Richard: There is an uneasy feeling, a feeling that there is a need to prop up a delusion.

Elena: Uneasy feeling—go there. WHO IS FEELING IT?

Richard: The uneasy feelings come from doubt. I don't doubt my experience but I am doubting the motivation for the rationalisation. Is it serving to hide/avoid something?

Elena: Not good enough. Go and look further. Look some more. Look. No "you". No. Seriously. No mysticism. Nothing special. Just no "you". Simple. Look.

Richard: I will. Whenever I catch myself thinking there is a self, I will look.

There are sensations.

Elena: Sensations are part of reality, yes. Who is feeling them?

Richard: There is a certain sense of heaviness/solidity in the chest area and the face, coolness on the skin, awareness of the movement of the abdomen.

Elena: Yes, all this is part of reality—body, sensations, yes. Who is feeling them?

Richard: There are audible thoughts, which imply that there is a self that is hearing, and visual thoughts that imply that there is a self that is seeing.

Elena: Thoughts, thought, no matter what the subject of the thought, thoughts are impersonal phenomena. They arise and pass away, some "I" thoughts, some other thoughts. WHO IS FEELING THEM?

Richard: For example as I am typing this sentence,

Elena: No, you are not typing any sentence. There is no "you". There's just the mind, and the body and the hands and the heart. Nothing owns it, there's no you doing it. Look.

Richard: There is an assumption that either I am dictating the sentence to my hands,

Elena: You are not dictating. And hands are, they are body phenomena. There is no "you".

Richard: Or that I am reading the words that are being typed.

Elena: "I" is reading? Where is the "I"? It's just a label.

Richard: When I pay closer attention,

Elena: You can't pay closer or not closer or very very close attention. You just can't. There is no "you". Attention is. No "you".

Richard: I realise that there is another option:

Elena: YOU CAN'T REALISE, THERE IS NO YOU. Realisation is. It's just a thought, a feeling.

Richard: The typing and reading are each just happening on their own.

Elena: Yes, and it's done through the body and the brain.

Richard: And indeed I find that my typing gets ahead of my reading.

Elena: Typing and reading are not yours. You did not buy them in a shop. You did not earn your life. And it wasn't 'given' to you. It's just life, happening. There is no "you". Look, it's just an imaginary label we habitually attach to every experience in reality.

Richard: Paying closer attention, I notice

Elena: Noticing is happening. Look again for what you call "I" here

Richard: That my fingers move

Elena: Your fingers?

Richard: on their own and it's all happening with precision and speed that would be difficult for me to replicate

Elena: For WHO to replicate?

Richard: if I consciously moved each finger and typed each letter.

Elena: THERE IS NO YOU. Look, Richard, I am serious. It's just a joke, do you hear, just a joke, this "I", "me".

Richard: Right now there are no particularly noticeable feelings.

Elena: Seriously, you are being lazy, weak—it's like you don't care. You just seem to like talking about spiritual stuff because it indulges you.

You need to decide if you're going to try and do this, because right now, it seems as if you don't care, you're not interested, and you're not up for investigating.

Give me your best shot now. Best simple looking at reality as it is. It's as simple as looking at your wife or girlfriend or mother. It's simple—you look and see that all this is Life living itself. Existence living itself. There is no "you" who is living this life. "You" is just a label.

A label, like a claim on experiences in reality. It's just a pointer, a label, nothing more than that—and it doesn't point to anything. You can see through it any time and nothing will change. Nothing. Life will continue to live itself. Nothing will change. There'll just be the seeing of reality as it is happens. You will just stay the same as you are now—all the good and bad and all the other stuff.

It just that it's not personal; there is no person, NONE. There is life happening in all these patterns. We use this label from our early years, and it's so sticky that it seems if it falls away, I will disappear. Nothing will disappear. If you drop the notion that Batman exists, what disappears? What? Nothing. Because it never existed. Same here. Look.

Drop all your assumptions about what liberation is. Read and FEEL what I gave you in the last couple of e-mails.

Take a good look and write to me tomorrow. Good night.

Richard: Thoughts of "I" are impersonal, HA! The gate was seen, reality is friction-less, no need to push things along, everything is where it should be, there are no doubts!

Elena: Tell me more. Do you think I'll fall for three lines of exclamation marks?

Richard: The mind is blank, like a deer in the headlights, as if it's saying "why are you asking me if something that isn't there is there?"

The thrill and the exhilaration have subsided, but the identification with the self is not there. Well, that might be putting it too strongly, but there is a clear sense that whatever there is, it's not self, it's something else. It's not always seen clearly as a thought or a sensation, but whatever it was, it's clear to the mind that it wasn't self.

Also, the mindfulness of the arising of the "I" sensations/thoughts is there, a certain vigilance. The Tibetan saying that mindfulness is like the grandparent watching a child just came to mind.

Elena: You could see that self is not there. And actually never has been, as you observed. The state will subside.

BUT

Life goes on, and since life was ALWAYS going on without "self", nothing will essentially change. There is nothing to change, right?

Check whether you still believe that there is a "you" that lives your life. What do you say?

Richard: Life is going on its own. No one is living it, but oh how easy it is to forget. While you're outside the movie hall, it's as plain as can be, but then a transparent screen comes down on top of reality and the movie starts playing again. The audience recalls that there is no self but is engrossed in the movie. A voice in the back keeps saying "this is not real", and the audience agrees. "Of course it's not—we're outside the movie hall. Now let's move on with our lives and help others get out of the movie hall!"

So, to answer your question, no. No one is living my life. But knowing/believing that is not enough, because the experience becomes like a recollection of a dream and ceases to be real.

Elena: You looked and saw there is no "you" living life; life just is. You saw that there is no self. If you really did, then you saw that self has never been there, ever.

So if self was never there in the first place, what happens to life now? If life has always lived without self, then it's not necessarily going to be any different. Essentially, nothing changes. All the conditioning is still in place, beliefs, limitations.

Do you see it?

Experience is real. Never being is real. You are not.

Is this true? If not, let's look at what is, based on your seeing.

Richard: It's been a couple of days now and things are settling in. It's clear in a very visceral and direct manner that the entire experience of living is impersonal, always was and always will be.

As you mentioned below, the conditioning, beliefs and limitations are still there, but the reflex to identify with things is no longer there. There is a sense of cool detachment, letting things be where they are, with no need to pull them or push them away. Reality is much more vivid and bright, and a sense of ease and contentment is emerging.

Experience is real, "me" and "I" are just labels for an amalgamation of thoughts and sensations that are always in flux. The dream I referred to is what "I" think you would call a state; in that state it's so obvious that there is no self, and outside that state there is knowing of it, but it's not immediate and direct. The same reality, but different perceptions of it.

See, it's not clear if you're saying that that there is only one way to perceive reality, and whether you're speaking from a position of direct perception or one of knowing. Nor is it clear where "I" should be at this point along that continuum to be considered "done" by your standards.

"I" feel like "I" have the "knowing" part down, and maybe it's just a matter of letting things deepen further for the "state" to become ever more present in daily life.

Elena: Ah. Good. You made me bring out the zen stick there, to strike you. Good. Great. Amazing.

You're right, it will all unfold. It's subtle. When you take the root out, all structures start to dissolve. In some the dissolving is subtle, in some it's like demolition. So you just go and live life, and enjoy unfolding.

Let's keep in touch, OK? Write any time.

Feelings and stuff will come up. Just look behind them and see what they really are. You will notice it all losing its weight and stickiness.

Whatever you're inspired to do—do it. Now you will do it from life living inspiration, not from the self looking to perfect itself. You know, enlightenment is about chopping wood, carrying water. It's not fancy.

Richard: Elena, many thanks for the effort and patience. This has been the most profound opening since I started in my practice. I agree with you that this is what the definition of Stream Entry should be. Without seeing no-self clearly, one can make progress, perhaps even profound progress, but "self" will keep messing things up and confusing whatever is seen or achieved.

Matt

Matt found me through my blog. I really enjoyed the conversation with Matt. It was very straightforward and clear. The seeing happened when I asked him directly about how it feels to be liberated. That was enough to dissolve the mind-created boundary between liberated and not liberated. It was beautiful to see him going through. And I'm delighted to share this conversation with you.—I. C.

Matt: Hello, Ilona,

I found your blog from a discussion on Facebook. Are you still available to have dialogues? I went to your "Start Here" page and wrote down "There is no self in reality at all." Here's my report:

- Felt peace, and at the same time excitement. Saw clear, continuous aliveness, uninterrupted by appearances. Sigh of relief.
- Digging deeper, I wrote down "Not even this relieved self, or peaceful perceiver of aliveness exists in reality." "NO PERCEIVER".
- Slight frustration, because that "doesn't make sense".
- What is this frustration protecting? If there is no self, there's no perceiver and nothing to protect.

- Doubt comes up that "I" can be enlightened and see through the separate "I". Laughter: that doesn't make sense either.
- What is doubt protecting? A sense that I could lose it and be out of control?
- This doubt and fear is part of the "I" belief. WHO has an "I" belief? Does an organic arising like a leaf or wave have an "I" belief?
- A leaf or wave has no belief, just momentary arising and falling of appearances within continuous aliveness.

That's how far I got.

Thanks so much,
Matt

Ilona: Thank you for writing to me. I'll help you work this out with all I've got.

Yes your doubt is spot on. "I" cannot get enlightened. But then, no I is necessary for anything to occur. Just in general—that's the point. Things are happening, there's no self making them happen, or controlling them, or experiencing them.

Ok. Imagine you are holding a spoon right now. Just imagine, how much does it weigh? What is it made of? Where did it come from? Is it part of a set? Take the time to do this. Really—I'm not kidding. Get as detailed as you can.

Then open your eyes and look. There is no spoon.

It is exactly the same with the self. There is no self. What you do is look: can it be found in real life? No, it's only imagined. You need to cut through this illusion until you see it clearly.

We need to look into thought. So let's start here: can you control thoughts? Can you stop them mid-stream? Can you know what the next thought will be? Where do thoughts come from? How does thinking work?

Just write everything that you feel is true. Let's see what you got.

Matt: "What you do is look: can it be found in real life? No, it's only imagined."

Yes, these appearing sensations and thoughts CANNOT be evidence of a separate self! It's just like the spoon. There were vivid sensations and qualities appearing when I was imagining it, but when I looked, nothing. Same with Matt. Thank you for the imaginary spoon metaphor. Brilliant.

"But you have been believing that there is a separate entity for whole your life, so it's not as easy as seeing that there is no spoon."

True. But can one half-second glimpse like that really cut through a lifetime of false belief? I don't know if there's a shift yet.

By the way, I am willing to repeat the "looking" and try harder. I don't know what your perspective is on "effortlessness". Some say that trying hard "re-engages the ego". I would guess you're not worried about that, since you say there is no such ego entity that could be re-engaged.

"We need to look into thought with thought. So let's start here: can you control thoughts?" No, even the belief that I can control thoughts is a thought, and I have no idea how that thought got here.

"Can you stop them in mid-stream?"

Impossible. Thoughts don't seem to have any duration anyway.

"Can you know what the next thought will be?"

Impossible. What an arrogant assumption I've harboured—that I'm in control of some future experience!

"Where do thoughts come from?"

Nowhere. Perhaps from some natural chemical reaction somewhere, but that's a thought too, and I don't see a concrete source for it.

"How does thinking work?"

Thinking seems to be a complex but empty functioning of a nervous system, like the dance of the bees. The "I"-thought claims agency, as if a thought can think thoughts. Bitter, grievous illusion! (small tears). Disgusting. Thank you.

Ilona: You are doing very well.

Yes, your answers about thought are spot on. Now we need to look at the content of thought and the labelling process itself.

Close your eyes and notice what is going on. Can you identify the feeling of aliveness, beingness, "am" that is always there, unchanging? Stay with this for a bit. Notice how breathing happens, and notice the sounds as breath moves in and out. Notice the mind labelling everything that is experienced:

Breathing comes, and the mind labels it, "I'm breathing." Hearing comes, and the mind says, "I hear." Feeling appears, "I feel…." Noticing is happening and the label comes: "I notice...."

Now, check to see if there is a real breather in there, a hearer, a feeler, a noticer.

Play with this for a bit and see what you find. Notice that "I" is just a word, a label that comes before other words or labels. "I" is just part of language.

Then open your eyes and look around. See things in the room: the word "table" points to a real table. The word "monitor" points to a real monitor. The word "body" points to a real body. The word "hand" points to a real hand.

Now look and see if there is "self" in real life. Can you find one? What does the word 'self' point to? Please write when you are ready.

Matt: "Breathing comes, and the mind labels it, 'I'm breathing.' Hearing comes, and the mind says, 'I hear.' Feeling appears, 'I feel...'"

Yes, it is all just labelling! Without labels, all that is just amorphous, nondescript clouds of sensation (if anything...). And the labelling is intimately connected to this "I" label, as if it is "I" that is seeing and inspecting these sensations and labels. And this "I" thought often seems to associate itself with the eyeballs-sensation. "Where am I? Behind the eyes."

But the eyes and the space behind are also just sensation-plus-assumption, and without labels, they are indescribable sensations that are actually hard to locate or pin down or describe in any way.

I can't find anything that is certain here; everything is shifting, dark, murky, jumbled. When I look for a breather, hearer and feeler, an image or a feeling is seen as if by these "closed eyes". I can't be an image or a feeling.

When I look for the seer of the image labelled "closed eyes", the "I" shifts to another kind of sensation or attitude or energy pattern that reminds me of my father somehow: another psychophysical image.

Then it seems that all of this is appearing on an open, airy movie screen that is not directly visible. Open, alive awareness. Am I not this open awareness? It is not a separate thing; it is one with whatever appears.

There is no separate "I" to be found—only sensations appearing in non-separate, open nothingness. Even though it is invisible it seems this no-thingness is alive, dynamic, clear. So ultimately, no, I can't find an entity that is doing breathing, hearing, feeling.

"I" is just a word/idea/experience seemingly behind all the other words, ideas and experiences. It is a convention of language that is believed, like the imaginary spoon. The word "spoon" is not a spoon. The word "I" is not a separate self.

"Noticing is happening and the label comes: 'I notice....'" Yes, there's that sense of ownership/agency/identity again, claiming its own separate existence.

"Then open your eyes and look around. See things in the room: the word table points to a real table. The word 'monitor' points to a real monitor. The word 'body' points to a real body. The word 'hand' points to a real hand. Now look and see if there is 'self' in real life. Can you find one? What does the word 'self' point to?"

It certainly doesn't point to anything that I can find. It is a false belief, blind faith, a bizarre 'religious cult' of suffering. The word "self" points to the word "self", that's it.

Ilona: Awesome, Matt. So is there a separate self at all? Was there ever?

Matt: No, it's logically impossible. That is the intellectual conviction here, superimposed on the cesspool of lethargy and ignorance. But I still need help!

Ilona: Haha, OK, no problem, let's get you to seeing. There is no self at all in real life. What feelings inside come up right now?

- Is there anything there trying to protect you? If so, what? What is behind the feelings?

- Look at the truth, accept it is truth and let the true reveal itself.
- Is there a "you" to see it?

Matt: "There is no self at all in real life. What feelings inside come up right now?"

I think a little bit sad; all the energy that went into building the "self" up, controlling him, making him stand out—all of that was a waste of time.

Ilona: Yes, it's sad. Just let that be OK.

Matt: Thank you SO much for saying that. It really IS OK that thoughts or energies labelled "sadness" flow through the open space of awareness.

Ilona: Yes, all was going on automatic anyway, just as it is now. There is no choice, no free will, all is life; all is flow, no matter how it may seem from a limited perspective.

Matt: YES, all is open flow, including the thoughts and labels that appear to be a "limited perspective".

"Is there anything trying to protect you? If so, what?"

Those feelings are about protecting 'specialness', arrogance, rightness.

Ilona: Look now, what is behind specialness?

Matt: Fear about not being special, not being "something", which is really fear of death.

Ilona: Yes, that which does not exist cannot die. Isn't that just crazy, how fear of death is constantly there, when there is nothing to die?

Matt: It's literally crazy; it's psychotic paranoia.

Ilona: Again, what is behind arrogance, what is behind rightness? Are they anything else but thoughts? If so, what is behind the thoughts?

Matt: Yes, all the above are indeed just thoughts and nothing else! Thoughts about thoughts, indicating nothing else but thoughts. Strangely, there seems to be a protective force against thriving—being totally alive and well and illumined.

Ilona: That is just programming, conditioning and conflicting beliefs; clutter in the system that does not let it run smoothly. I call it the iVirus. It's just a set of data in the system that needs to be removed so the system can run freely. What is behind it?

Matt: iVirus, yes! And looking will "remove" it. Behind all of these data (and others, if they come up), is the interpretation or "point of view" of separate self. A point of view is not solid, separate; it is transparent to awareness, aliveness, beingness. Points of view are no problem.

Ilona: When a point of view is taken for reality, it's a problem. As long as you know that the point of view is just a story, it stops having power. It dissolves.

Also, write down what you expect from this. Sometimes a subtle belief can be in the way. Just get it all out in writing.

Matt: I expect from "looking"' to see very clearly, with certainty and permanence, that there is no separate, substantial I-self. Then I hope to be forever happy and humble and generous and loving (and spiritually successful and special!)—it all comes back to the belief in an individual "I", and the hope of "enlightening the I".

There is nothing I've found yet that exists so that it can be enlightened. I have nothing to substantiate the belief that there is a real "person" here. No proof whatsoever. Just an old story. Yes, the story has no power if there is no belief feeding it.

Ilona: Good, look at the truth, accept it as truth and let the truth reveal itself. It really helps at this point to get out into nature and observe totality. Just spend some time in a park.

Nature can be found everywhere. You are not outside of it. Keep looking and just notice the obvious.

Matt: Thank you. I was able to look deep and long while walking through the city.

"Look at the truth, accept it as truth and let the truth reveal itself."

The truth is, I have looked and I have not yet been able to locate a separate "me". When there seems to be a "me", it's clearly not a "me", but a mere story made of sensation and thought. Ilona, when am I going to be satisfied and give up trying to locate this non-existent entity?!

Ilona: Is there a 'you' to see it?

Matt: There is no "me" trying to locate a non-existent entity! There is no "me" looking for "me". There is no "me" typing a message. There is no "me" who believes in empty stories.

Much gratitude.

Ilona: Awesome stuff, Matt. I see that it's almost there, last few steps.

Matt: Yes, so, let's let the fairy tale end!

Ilona: After seeing through illusion, life does not change, it's the same as always been, "chop wood, carry water..." What changes is the feeling inside. There is freedom in every experience. Freedom to feel, to express, to live, to enjoy. It's freedom to feel anger and not be consumed by it.

The happy ending is the end of loops of judgement feeding on themselves.

...So don't expect life to suddenly transform. It will over time. With every belief dropped there will be more and more peace in the head. Again, "specialness" is the quality of a human infected with the iVirus. Once it's removed, then specialness goes too. There comes the ordinarily simple human being. And peace within with what is.

Matt: Beautiful.

Ilona: I see that it's almost there, just a few final steps. Let it settle a bit, live through the day just noticing the obvious, and answer me a few questions. Firstly:

Is there a self in any shape or form in reality? Was there ever?

Matt: "Self" is a just label, a habitual thought. Although the habit is still strong, this thought has no form that I can locate or substantiate. Thought has no shape or form in reality. There is no separate self that has any shape or form in reality. There is no one who has a habitual thought. Thoughts without a thinker. Sensations without a sensor.

Ilona: Explain in detail how the self works and what it is.

Matt: The "self" doesn't "work" at all, it only appears to exist and function. The self is empty of self. The functioning of a non-existing entity is non-existent, empty. Thoughts of separateness have no duration or real existence of their own. Thought is empty of itself.

Only Existence exists through the apparent thoughts and sensations that appear to describe separateness. These thoughts and sensations appear to appear and simultaneously disappear, revealing only the Open Space of Aware Existence.

The thought or sensation that says "self" is not even thought and sensation; it is nothing other than the Open Space of Aware Existence Itself.

Ilona: How does it feel to be liberated?

Matt: Exactly the same as ever, only sweeter because there is no anxiety around those feelings. There is no anxiety about "becoming liberated". There is no desire for a different state.

Ilona: Oh, yes! I see that you are through!

Matt: Strong doubts and reservations arise, but they are also empty, without substance or power.

Ilona: They will keep arising for a while. It's not the end of thought, or doubt. It's the dawn of truth, and as you stay on the truth, stay with it, they will weaken. You know that, so just keep looking behind stuff.

Matt: Thank you, you are so kind.

Ilona: Sweet! I'm so happy for you. Welcome to living free! So, what was it that made you realise? Anything in particular?

Matt: Nothing in particular! Nothing really happened, and everything is exactly the same as before: I'm still grumpy and lazy, etc.—it's just that all this is clearly beside the point. Maybe it was when you asked, "How does it feel to be liberated?" That question was not directed at the mind, and I gently noticed there was never any boundary between "liberated" and "not yet liberated".

The mind always looks for some non-existent boundary, and is expecting some special experience or bliss. But even that silly tendency is okay. Everything is the same, but everything is okay.

Ilona: Good one! Matt, thank you very much for looking. It is a real pleasure to meet you.

Matt: You are a pleasure, and a miracle—giving anonymous people your time, not charging people money or claiming something special about yourself. Just patiently asking people to look for themselves. Bless you!

Ilona: Thank you. Big smile here. By the way, could you expand a bit on "sweeter"? Do you notice anything else different in everyday life? Can you talk about it more, please?

Matt: "Sweeter" is vividly felt when I'm writing this, focusing on these facts. It's like "being at home" with everything exactly as it already is. It's a sweet miracle that everything can appear while being without substance.

The "feeling" of sweetness seems to ebb and flow. But the sweetness is not merely a feeling—it's deeper than that. All of us are already at home in liberation, even in our suffering. That's paradoxically sweet, or maybe bitter-sweet.

Ilona: So much appreciation…

Matt: So much appreciation for the sweetness we call "Ilona" and for her selfless communication.

Love forever.

Ilona: Love forever.

Brian

Brian was a seeker from the non-duality path, struggling emotionally. We rolled out the old "Santa metaphor"—it's a good 'un—and he saw through the illusion of "I" very quickly. Gratitude is one of the hallmarks of "crossing the gate", and he expressed it to his childhood teacher whom he suddenly remembered very vividly.—E. N.

Brian: Hello, Elena, I hope this e-mail finds you well.

A friend of mine told me about your blog after her recent interaction with you.

If you would, please help me to stop struggling with I/ego/self. I get it… intellectually and have had periods of quiet/understanding/peace but… BUT the whole thing reverts to programming and pain and ugh… I get so frustrated and… well… you know how the stories go.

Elena: Hi, Brian. Thanks for reaching out.

What is "I" for you?

Brian: I am not sure.

From reading the texts on non-duality (Gita, Krishnamurti, Nisargardatta, Maharshi etc.), the "I" doesn't exist. It is a fabrication built on experiences that are taken to be real and out of that... poof! I emerges with its likes and dislikes and its preferences and preoccupations. I get that on an intellectual level... but...

But for me, the "I" still feels the hurt of parental criticism, the insecurity of unemployment/a job interview and anger/frustration/confusion when its kid does not excel in sport. "I" is angry often times as it is also envious and revengeful in thought.

"I" feels unworthy. "I" is critical and judgemental. "I" doesn't know what to do and "I" goes in circles.

"I" could go on and on... and it does.

After replying to your e-mail I went to your blog and read your latest entry. Here in the US in the 90s it was common to see these "hidden" pictures for sale in the mall. When you looked at them, you saw nothing, but if you would look just right... an image would be seen. I would stare and stare while those around me would do the same and then they would go, "oh, I see... how cool!" and I am like, "what, what! I don't see anything!" I thought it was a joke. Then one day I saw one but then moved my head and it was gone. That's what this whole seeking/searching thing seems like to me at times.

Elena: If you want to see, you stop reading and look.

Hurt? What's that? Emotion. Emotion is a wave in a consciousness. "You"—a label that assigned AFTER the experience. Look.

Take that emotion and go behind it. What's there?

Brian: Yes, I've put the books away.

You are saying hurt feelings are emotions and emotions are just waves in consciousness. Additionally, I label these emotions (waves) AFTER the actual experience.

You want me to see what's there behind the emotion.

Thinking... thinking... what's there behind the emotion? There is nothing I can see behind, next to, under or over the emotion; the emotion is just there and I feel it.

More thinking… more asking myself what is behind it.

I guess I could also answer with… I am behind the emotion but I am frankly not sure. I feel circular again, because now I want to ask who the hell am I and I don't know!

Or… behind the emotion is fear. Or is that just another emotion?

OK, I am sending this off now but I will continue to think on this because I don't think the responses I gave are what you are looking for.

Elena: Fear? Look up behind the fear. Bow to the amazing creation of consciousness—fear. Invite fear closer and peek behind it.

Brian: I don't see anything behind fear. It's empty space. I can see things I create on the surface of fear, lots and lots of things. But fear itself just seems to be there, or it seems to come and go.

Also, it seems far less personal now. I get the sense it is not personal at all unless I want to make it that way.

This is what comes back when looking behind fear.

Elena: Bingo. So see that it's all impersonal phenomena. We were just conditioned from early childhood to assign "I" to all that is happening—feelings, thoughts, body, etc.

There is no "I" in reality. "I' is just a label. Look.

Brian: I've been looking and all that was seen was a great big "I". "I" here, "I" there, "I" seemingly everywhere.

This morning, while I was sitting, I was looking again and then the words came to mind: "look behind 'I'".

I am just telling you what came to mind or what I saw in my mind when I looked behind "I".

I was standing there. Behind I was a very dark grey doorway with no door and beyond the doorway was empty space, rather like a picture of outer space.

For what it is worth, "things" have seemed less personal the last few days. My daughter threw a big rude insult the other day, one that would usually get me pretty agitated, but for whatever reason, this one, well I didn't care so much. There was still a need to discuss being rude to people, but as far as taking it personally, I didn't. Sometimes I think I am still waiting to get mad about it but there is nothing there.

As far as I goes… not sure what will happen there. It would be great to see this feeling rise or that thought rise without being attached to it.

Elena: Nice. You are doing great, Brian.

There is no "I". It's a thought. There are emotions, sensations, feelings, the body—all exist. If "I" was real, why is it not real in the small baby that just opens its eyes and look at the world around without any "I" thought?

See that "I" is not real, It's made up label, a thought. A thought so innocent, but so persistent, that all life springs from being a separate entity. Keep looking deeper.

Brian: Looking continues but the "I" remains. I still sense emptiness behind the "I", but the "I" still stands proudly in the doorway. The "I" still seems very real.

I will continue to look deeper.

Elena: Look, if I told you to find Santa in the room, what would you say to me?

Right, you will say that Santa is an illusion, that he does not exist in reality. What are the components of Santa that exist in reality?

The thought of Santa.

Feelings of Santa (maybe "heart-warming").

Sensations (maybe "fuzzy").

But there is no actual Santa existing in reality.

If I told you to find the self, you can find a thought of self.

A feeling of self.

Sensations.

All that is real and exists in reality.

Can you find the self? Isn't it just as vague and illusive as Santa? Yep, because it does not exist in reality. It's a label, illusion, construct.

Look.

Brian: Why didn't you just tell me I was Santa in the first place! (grin, or is it "Ho Ho Ho!"?)

So in reality there are feelings and sensations. These come and go; sometimes like a light breeze and sometimes with the force of a hurricane. But behind them is nothing but still air.

I am that still air. The illusion of I is to think you are lifted by a warm summer breeze or pounded by a cold winter blast. Without the illusion there are still summer breezes and winter blasts but there has always been and always will be still air.

The confusion was in the feelings of and sensations of... "I". Those are rather persistent, changing and very real and an easy mistake to be made. It also explains why I couldn't really be found when looked for... just the feelings of and sensations of "I" were found.

Merry Christmas, Elena!

Santa

Elena: Ho ho ho! Merry Christmas!

That was awesome!

Is there a "you" in any shape or form in reality?

Brian: No, the thought of "I/you/me" is shapeless and formless. It can appear to have form or shape, as a beam of light through a window will illuminate smoke from a cigarette and seem to give it form, but when you run your hand through it, there is nothing there.

In reality, phenomena (thoughts, feelings or a Santa!) can illuminate and seemingly give form and shape to what we think of (thought of in some cases) as I/you/me, but like the smoke, it is an illusion.

Elena, my dear, a memory has just arisen.

In High School I had a teacher. I was warned by most kids who had her before: "Be careful, she is a tough one!" And other types of worrisome warnings. The class was literature. While she was demanding and strict, "sit straight in your chair!" it took only a few weeks for me to begin to realise there was something very special about her. She cared and it showed.

Looking back now I can see what she was doing: she was gently trying to wake sleeping souls. One book we read was "Waiting for Godot". I still remember how she particularly liked that book. That's the memory that just came to mind while typing.

In her class we would take turns reading aloud, and then as a group, led by her, we would discuss it. I, too, began to have an appreciation for this work and for her. Just for fun, I went over and read a few quotes from the book just now; how appropriate they are to our conversation. After reading them again now, I really see how special she and those like her, like you, Elena, are.

The following quote is from Samuel Beckett's "Waiting for Godot".

"But that is not the question. Why are we here, that is the question. And we are blessed in this, that we happen to know the answer. Yes, in this immense confusion one thing alone is clear. We are waiting for God to come."

I saw her obituary in the local paper in the late 1990s and I remember feeling sad and regretful that I never stopped by to thank her and tell her how much I appreciated her.

Now...now I just did!

Time for Santa to make his rounds!

Elena: Oh, Brian, thank you for the amazing story. This play is so intricate, it makes me appreciate every little detail, everything as an amazing creation, amazing.

Do you mind, dear friend, if I ask you couple of questions which you should answer clearly and precisely, looking at your immediate experience?

You are saying there is no "you". Was there any "you" before?

What's changed?

Is anybody living life?

Brian: Who is asking? (ha ha ha) I bet you get that a lot.

Was there a "me" before? You mean before I saw that "me" was just an illusion that never was? I'm not sure… ha ha ha! Oh, it's all so stupid, yet funny.

What's changed? It's not personal. Last night's sleep was interrupted by many recognitions of previous thoughts of me, me, me in various situations and just how silly/obvious (words are hard to find here) it all was. The searching… it's like water asking, "am I wet?" Humour asking, "am I funny?"

I think the next big thing will be self-help books for rivers. They will have chapters on "healing your inner stream" and "learning to go with the flow" and "is the ocean really your destiny?" Ha ha ha.

Also, the conditioning and the habits of old seem much clearer and much weaker. I get the sense they will begin to fall away. I feel lighter. Words work on the surface but are rather useless deep down. The bumper sticker "Shit Happens" has taken on a much deeper meaning… ha ha ha.

I heard once that you and I are really just God's way of experiencing his creation. Consciousness's way of seeing its self and experiencing creation. Beautiful.

Is anybody living life? Hmmm, let me ask my dog and get back to you on that one. He has proven pretty reliable on these sorts of things… ha ha ha. He said, "No" but the cat just laughed at the question. ha ha ha.

You and I had been working together for just about a week. I would read your e-mail response in the morning and then sit with it and… look or whatever it is you would like to call it. There was some progress I can see now, I didn't see it then.

I first saw feelings and sensations for what they were but the "I" remained firmly entrenched. Then yesterday I sat before reading your e-mail.

It was an emotion-filled sitting. I saw the younger me, the hurt me, the seeking, efforting me. I could say to myself, "it's OK and I am sorry they hurt you, they were wrong to do that, you have done a great job dealing with it all and I will be that big brother you always wanted, the caring supporting parent you wanted, I will help you", and it was genuine and tears rolled; the body shook. I then said or the thought arose (however you want to say it) "I want to come home, I want to come home now."

The timer sounded and then the cat started rubbing his face on my hand. "Okay, the cat is here now", I said to myself, and spent a few minutes with him. I then got up, turned off the timer and saw your e-mail on my phone and read it.

Of course!

I'm Santa!

Usually I give your words some time to float around and sink in, but this time there was no need. I went right to the computer and you know the response.

So how did "it" happen? That's right! Ha ha ha.

Happening happens.

Gladly accepting your thank you and hugs!

Elena: That's right, that's right.

I am glad I was able to help.

But but but.

I need clear answers to confirm that you've seen the real deal.

Once seen—never unseen.

I need to know that for sure, otherwise I will continue to ask you.

So again,

Do you exist?

Were you there?

Thanks.

Brian: No and no. Was there a "me" before? You mean before I saw that "ME" was just an illusion THAT NEVER WAS?

Elena: Nice.

Dave

The conversation with Dave was the first one I had through our new site—www.liberationunleashed.com. The turning point was when Dave had a proper look at the witness. It is so common to believe that "me" is the witness, when in reality there is only witnessing happening. It was a pleasure to guide Dave.—I. C.

Ilona: Hi. Let's start with you describing where exactly you are at the moment. Do you exist?

Dave: Do I exist?

I know there is no me. Never has been, never will be. I've done enough work or thinking/meditating on this to really know this is the truth. But then "I" get trapped by negative thoughts. I'm sure you've heard this hundreds of times, maybe thousands! It's "understanding" that there is no such thing as "me", but I can't seem to get "to" the gate, never mind passing through it... I don't exist as a separate entity, no.

In reading one of the posts on the Gate, someone said, "So you understand the concept but have not seen it." I think that describes where I am. What a great site!

Ilona: I know exactly where you are. Staring at the gate, not sure how to cross. Problem is—there is no you to cross. Crossing happens by itself when seeing happens. And although there's no you to see, no you is necessary for seeing to occur... so look. Investigate reality.

Is there a witness or is witnessing happening? Tell me what you've got.

Dave: Is there a witness or is witnessing happening?

Hmmm... I'm truly not sure. I feel there is a witness watching all this happen, but that may be due to my Buddhist background? Maybe this is a sticking point for me. If there is no "me", then "who" is witnessing?

I'm feeling "yes and no", and I know that is not really a great answer, but that is what is coming.

Ilona: Look here, there is reading happening, focusing happening, seeing happening. What is behind all this? Is there a separate entity watching this? Or is it just a thought passing by: "I am witnessing..."

Can "I" do anything?

Answer when you are 100% sure.

Dave: Ha! Of course! There is just another thought, "'I' am witnessing", no different than, "'I' am writing", "'I' am walking", "'I' am breathing", "I am bad", good, etc."... When you put it that way, it's so obvious.

Perfect.

Ilona: So is there a you as a separate entity at all? Was there ever? What is the "I", then?

Dave: "So is there a you as a separate entity at all?"

No, there never really was a separate entity. "I" was given a name, told I was a boy, sometimes good, sometimes bad, "I" was conditioned to believe in a separate "me" by my family, teachers, friends and society... and, of course, I had no reason not to believe in "me" at that point.

"Was there ever?"

No. Looking back, I know that now. The conditioning runs SO deep, right through the bones. People, places, events "appear", but as a separate entity, "I" have never really been there.

Maybe that's why we feel the same inside as our bodies age. We don't feel different inside 'cause there is no one there inside to feel any different. I've always felt that way, but never looked at it from that "view"... or "no view".

"What is the 'I', then?"

The "I" is a bundle of thoughts and conditioning. Though, when in emotional or physical pain, it sure feels as if there is an "I" experiencing it. (which is what I'm going through now). It feels that way when "I" take the pain "personally", which I tend to do, even when I "know" there is no one that the pain is happening to.

I know it's just "pain happening", and I need to get past the taking it as a personal "I". I know the pain will still be there, but will be much reduced when I know, really know, that's it's just pain, happening to no one.

I hope I didn't over-explain my point, Ilona...

Ilona: No, no, it's great. Just rant about everything.

So how does it feel to be liberated?

Dave: If you're asking me, personally how it feels to be liberated, I don't know. I don't believe I am there yet. If you're asking, as I've heard you ask before, what liberation should feel like:

A liberated human behaves like all of "us" but is not attached to anything that happens. Events come and go, and though some can be seen as good or bad, to the liberated, they are simply events "happening". Neither good nor bad, nor necessarily do they have much to do with him/her. There's no one to judge.

I guess from my perspective, that's what it should be like. Life's events don't stop happening... life is living itself, as a matter of fact, quite well, from the perspective of being truly free of the self. As Buddha said so well, "Deeds are being done, but there is no doer." Life is being lived, but there is no "one" living it.

You gave me permission to rant, so this is how I feel this moment, Ilona...

I want peace. Real, everlasting peace. Freedom from this treadmill of self-ing. It's so tiring and pitiful, actually. I want to be free of judging and seeing myself in a negative light. Sometimes I wish I knew nothing of this, then I wouldn't beat myself up over my suffering as I should "know" better. Is ignorance bliss? I don't want to think so.

I know it's a form of insanity or craziness to believe both things at the same time, but that is where I am. The times that I am in the "no me" zone are the, happiest most freeing times of my life. Then I drift back to the "real" world (problems, self-pity, bills, etc., etc.) and it all comes back. You said it PERFECTLY once: "The world is real, YOU are not." Simple, yet perfect. Why can't I hold on to this?

Why can't this TRUTH "stick"? I know what you're going to ask, as I've sort of "studied" your writings...

"What is the fear that is keeping me stuck... what's behind the fear..."

Ilona: It's OK, all good, almost there. This is happening. Just notice. There is no you to believe thoughts. Thoughts like "this is bad", "this is good" or "this is how it should be" are simply appearing and disappearing effortlessly. There is no you to think them. There is no you to believe them. There is no you that is crying for help.

This has nothing to do with belief.

Tell me what can be known 100% right now. Look at thoughts and Notice: thoughts are real, the content isn't.

And yes, what is behind that fear? Allow that fear to just be there. Is there a you to even allow it?

Notice how all is just happening. Trusting this process is surrendering.

Dave: I will answer your questions, but I wanted to share something with you that happened recently. I'd been dating this woman for close to a year and we recently decided to end the relationship. I've been having a tough time with it, till our talk. Whether it's through us working together, I'm not sure...

But for the first time in a while, I really feel OK about the situation. It just hit me that "this is perfectly OK... any sadness you feel is nothing more than a thought, completely unreal."

Who is there to be sad? It was a very strange, almost an "out of body" experience, cause for the first time, I felt like there really, truly, was "nobody home". No one to be hurt. I went to bed feeling that way and sure enough, I feel the exact same way right now as I write this at 8:45 am. I'm very happy about it, but not in a "Yay! Look what 'I've' done", or "look how far 'I've' come" way. I's sort of a quiet "non-event". Not sure how to deal with it, but I do like this feeling or way of "being"...

I know that's a bit off topic, but I HAD to share...

Thank you, Ilona.

Ilona: It's not off topic at all. This story is here as a natural flow of things.

It's great to hear that there is "nobody home" to get upset... this is great. All that does not serve anymore is starting to fall off, and all that is true is falling into place. Trust that. I call this process Falling.

There is nothing to hold on to and no one to hold on. All is just happening.

Thank you for sharing. Now back to the questions.

Dave: "Tell me what can be known 100% right now. Look at thoughts and notice: thoughts are real, the content isn't."

What can be known 100% is that our life is made of thoughts and you do not have to believe them. I've noticed that a LOT today as I really paid attention since I've had that "breakthrough" yesterday that I talked to you about.

Every time something came up, for instance... "Why did we break up? Did I do something wrong? Why did this happen?" When I step back and look at those feelings and what is behind them, I find they are nothing but thoughts. Completely made up in my head, from who knows where? It takes the personal sting out of them immediately.

Things "happened". Just like how the sun came out today, then it rained a bit. No difference. I'm a little dishevelled as I don't know why I don't feel any connection to the pain, this is very new.

Yes, thoughts are real. You can't deny that, as they constantly come and go. It's when we create the stories around the content and believe them that the stories seem real. We give them their life. It seems I've been spending my entire life believing in a lie... a fiction... a "woe is me" sad story. (at least that's "my" story... and I'm not sticking to it!)

And yes, what is behind that fear?

I'm afraid of losing the "progress" that I've "seemingly" made. I feel I'm "really getting it" this time and my fear is that I'll somehow slip back... maybe for no reason or something perceived as "bad" or "upsetting" will happen and I'll revert back to the "poor me" story. I don't want that. I don't want to go back there. (I know there is really no "there" to go, but I'm sure you know what I mean.)

I somehow feel "safe" here talking with you and like-minded people, but "out there" in the world, I want to still live from the place of "nobody home". I'm hoping you have a support type system in place in case of slipping back... Do you ever slip back once you feel you really "know it"? Does it stay?

"Allow that fear to just be here. Is there a you to even allow it?"

When I allow the fear to be there, it goes right to your second sentence. I feel there is no me to allow it. Right now I feel so secure in my "knowing". I don't have to do anything. It's right here, where it's always been. Sometimes I find myself laughing out loud at how obvious it is (I am right now...).

Still... I have the little devil on my shoulder that whispers that this won't last. Actually, that's not completely true. The little devil is NOT there whispering doubts in my ear, but I "imagine" that he is going to show up at some point. Maybe this is the remnant of "me" trying to hold on? Could that be it?

"Notice how all is just happening. Trusting this process is surrendering."

That's exactly what I need to do. Trust. Trust this process. (which I do!) I told a friend of mine today that I've made more progress in knowing who I really am in the past week than I have in over 25 years of meditating. I don't say that lightly, as I love my meditation practice. I still do... in fact, my meditation is even better without "me". It's much deeper and by not giving my thoughts the attention they want makes it much more efficient as well.

Where do I go from here, Ilona? How do I trust more? Just by "trusting" I take it? How can I be sure this is real and is going to stay? There a lingering doubt of this lasting way back in the dark corner of my conditioned mind.

Ilona: You are right here, looking at it. Now just a final push. Look for yourself, is it true that there is no "me"? Let the truth be revealed.

Once you find out that Santa is not real, can you believe that he is real again? Doubt can come up and it does. But what has been seen, can never be unseen. And yes, we have an aftercare group—this is like a whole new world to explore, and you don't have to do it alone.

So... how does it feel to be liberated?

Dave: "Look for yourself, is it true that there is no 'me'? Let the truth be revealed."

Of course there is not a real "me". Right now, that sounds ridiculous... I mean, what would a real "me" look like? Santa Claus is a great analogy. Once you "know" he's not real, how could you believe in him again? You would not be sincere if you said you did. How could there possibly be a me?

When you look at it in the right way, right between the eyes, no religion, no beliefs, no bullshit... where is it? It is NOT. I Am NOT. Yet I am everything. No separation. I'm saying things I've read but never believed or "got", but now I don't have to believe, because I fucking (sorry) KNOW.

How did you come up with this "direct way" of guiding people? Why does it sometimes take Zen people as well as others YEARS AND YEARS to get this? I know why it took me... but what about people who have "given their life" to their "Masters", for what? For promises of Liberation... always an arm's length away?

What do you do that is so different? I've always heard that when you finally "get it", you shouldn't be surprised that "nothing changes, but in the way you look at the world, everything changes."

"So how does it feel to be liberated?"

Just like that last statement. My bills are still there, I'm still by myself, I still live where I live, my job is the same... yet I "see" it all from a completely different perspective. Why aren't I feeling the same sadness and self-pity?

I don't get it... it HAS to be that I've finally realised that there is NO ME to feel that way. I feel light and sort of carefree... it may sound strange, but I don't really care or feel "personally connected" to whatever comes. Whatever comes, comes. The End. I don't control life. Who the hell am I to think that I can control anything that happens? Are you kidding me? I don't have and don't want that kind of power.

I think that if I re-read any of the classic texts, like The Tao De Ching, or Ramana Maharshi, I feel that instead of being lost, I could actually "understand" what they were talking about. This is life altering.

I have to ask again: will this "stick". Do I need, as you say, "after-care"? I would not want to lose this freedom, maybe I can't. It's too new, I don't really know. What do you recommend I do? I would love to help people once I am "stabilised". How can I not pay forward what you have "shown"?

Ilona: Thank you! Your answer is really touching.

What is different in what we do? Well, we bring clarity to the gate. You can't deepen a freedom you don't have—many traditions and teachers try to deepen their students free. That doesn't work. The student has to be free before the freedom can expand.

And then of course—I make you look for yourself. It's not about believing this or believing that. It's not even about training to look—a baby doesn't need training to open its eyes, so why should we?

That's enough to break the wall. One look and it's over.

Yes, we have an amazing aftercare group and it REALLY helps to speak to people who went through the same thing, because doubt comes up. It takes time to settle, to rebalance the system so it can run smoothly.

Nothing to fear about, nothing to lose. It's a period of falling...

So for the end of this conversation can you answer these few questions:

Is there a "you" in any shape or form at all?

What was that last push for you?

What is this "self" and how does it work?

What would you say to somebody who came to this for first time and had never heard about it?

Dave: "I make you look for yourself. That's enough to break the wall. One look and it's over."

Of course! Anyone truly liberated through the ages has always said things like, "it's closer than your breath", "you already are, but don't know it"... I have to say, and this is only "my" opinion, but having someone there who "knows" to guide you makes all the difference in the world. Yes, you have to look for yourself, but having someone "point" out where to look and what look for is the difference... at least to "me" (not).

On a side note, my depression has lifted. This is a sort of therapy, maybe another facet of what you do?

"Is there a you in any shape or form at all?"

No, and I see there never was. And life runs much better and more smoothly without "me" in the way. I "thought" there was. Now I've "seen" through that illusion. There's really nothing to add.

"What was that last push for you?"

Sort of early on, when you asked "is there a witness? Or is witnessing happening?", I gave you the answer that I really didn't know. I said something like, "it seems like there is both".

Then you, not letting me off the hook that easily, said, "is it just a thought passing by, I am witnessing... Can I do anything?" That was when it all really "hit" me and I "knew" I was really getting it, for the first time. At that point it all seems so obvious, it was almost funny...

Maybe the final push was when I allowed the fear to be there, and realised that no, there isn't a "me" to allow the fear... then it got very funny as it was so completely obvious and so simple, obviously simple enough to overlook after a lifetime of seeking.

"What is this 'self' and how does it work?"

The 'self' is a bundle of conditioning from parents, school, friends and society that tells you "who" you are, what to believe. And very soon, you do. When you believe your thoughts, both good and bad, you create the "self", with all its fears, insecurities, as well as "I'm better than everyone else at whatever".

This "self", when believed, runs your life, controls your actions and decisions... when the truth is, only when you "let go" of the "self" are you TRULY in control. By "control", I mean you allow things to happen as they do, you don't try to control anything, then you're not "controlled".

You don't take life's "events" personally. It wants you to believe it's protecting you by feeding off your fear... and let's face it, there's enough fear to go around for everyone, if you choose to believe it. Anything that happens in nature is not personal. Anything that happens in Life is unique, but not personal. Why should it be any different? Because of "self" and "thoughts".

If I had to share this with someone? What I've already told my best friend. If you're still searching, you need to go to this site, or Marked Eternal first, read the work she is doing there... go over the Start Here page and answer the questions yourself. It doesn't cost a thing. That's a big plus, when you see there is no money "scam" thing going on.

I'd just say—give it a chance! You've got nothing to lose (except "you"!), which I do not say at first... I just tell them that I've found an inner peace and in this short time I've seen how life can just "flow" if you get "you" out of the way and just let it.

I hope I've answered that question in the way you were asking, Ilona. I wasn't really sure.

I feel really good. A little nervous, as I said, of "back-sliding". I want to tell people, but most of my friends would not really understand, I believe.

All I can say is thank you very much! Where do "I" go from here?

Ilona: This is just perfect! I'm delighted for you. I love your clarity. I'm feeling lots of appreciation here.

Please join our group and stick around. There will be questions and doubts and all sorts of other stuff as part of falling, but you are through and from now on, life gets interesting.

Thank you for sending your friend here. It's a real pleasure to assist in this. If you get interested in learning some tips on guiding, you are very welcome to join our team. It's not magic.

But for now, just rest, let it settle. Enjoy the ride! Woo hoo!

Dave: Thank you Ilona! You were great!

Peter had been meditating for long a time: Transcendental Meditation, Zen, Vipassana. When I asked what he was looking for from our work, he said that he was seeking to live in the present moment. We saw that the present moment is the only thing that is, and that it's not necessary to seek it.—E. N.

Peter: Could you work with me one on one on using the Direct Pointing method? I'd be very grateful. Time may be a bit erratic as I'm busy at summer school. But I'll make time.

Elena: Sure. Erratic is good for me since I am also a little busy, but will make time for you. I love the way you expressed gratitude right from the beginning. How could I not help?!

I propose the following. While we chat, I would like you to try not to read any internet discussion board, and put the books aside—spend your time on looking. That's why we are here together, and let's make it productive. Deal?

Peter: Hi, Elena. Yes. Ok. Thank you for agreeing to do this.

Well, I've been spending some time looking over the last week or so and would like to try and take it further through this practice of dialogue. I think I may get further with that method than I'm able to through simple self-reflection, so I think I should give it a try.

What I'm finding is that there are times when I'm aware of an absence when I look for the self. There's a "nothing" there, which is surprising in a way.

For example, as if I were to walk around all day thinking I had money in my pocket and I went to pay for something and found—OK, no money. It's a little disorienting and there are some physical sensations that go with it.

So quite often when I look for the self, that's my experience. And it's not completely new, I've noticed it before on and off but it's not something that I've specifically cultivated. I've noticed it during practices like Vipassana but also in daily life.

Elena: Tell me, what are you searching for? Take a good look at it and write exactly you are searching for.

Peter: To live in the present moment. It sounds like a cliché but I do believe that's what I'm searching for.

Elena: So what's missing?

Peter: I may be in fact living in the present moment, but a lot of the time my behaviour doesn't reflect that. It's often dominated by stories: thoughts of the present or past. Fantasy, worry, rumination. So I don't know if it's something missing or something "extra" which is there.

Elena: See that there is only the present moment. Nothing else. All the other stuff you mention is thoughts/feelings. Is this true?

I do need answers from the neck down only. Before you answer anything—drop your mind into the heart. Then take a good look. Only then write.

Peter: I spent some time looking. What I found was that each time I looked, there was a shift. So if I kept doing the looking, this feeling became continuous and like a state. Like the sound of a bell struck again and again eventually becoming continuous. This lasted for a few hours. Is this what you mean?

Elena: No.

My question is very simple: what is it that you are looking for here, in your practice, in this work we are doing right now? Anything you want to achieve? What's missing from you right now?

Peter: Of course. As far as spiritual practices, I've been meditating for a long time, but not rigorously! I started with Transcendental Meditation when I was in my teens (I'm now in my forties). It was a very positive experience for me although my experience with the organisation itself was not so positive.

I think the main thing was that it was a very happy meditative absorption that helped me with stress. It was an introduction to bliss and those things. I think after a while I stopped making progress with it and so lost motivation.

Ultimately I moved on to more Buddhist types of meditation, Zen and more recently Vipassana. I became more interested in these things a couple of years ago and since then I've had some fresh results that have motivated me to investigate further:

I'd never had a lot of success with breath meditation (preferring mantras) but suddenly this became easier, and I experienced a sense of the breath as being quite separate from my body—of occupying a space that was not confined to the body and not even particularly attached to "my body".

After reading Daniel Ingram's book I began to notice impermanence much more easily. Also, I became more aware of experiences taking place in a no-self type of space. So for example the sensation of walking would easily break down into very fine granules of sensation, like snowflakes.

And it became clear that these granules were coming and going on their own with no effort from me, and that in fact they weren't attached to anything called a "me" either. I also started to become aware of the arising and passing of these events in an ongoing flow, and of the space around these events.

Shortly after that point, I became more aware of a "nothing". I don't know how else to describe it but it's a feeling of an absence rather than a presence that I get sometimes. I'm sure it's always been there but for some reason I see it now, whereas I didn't before.

Sometimes I have the experience of an observer, like a camera recording my entire experience. Other times (and this is quite difficult to explain!) it's like the camera and the viewed object are one, or else there are an infinite number of "cameras" of awareness saturating through all phenomena.

I usually get this after practising some inquiry-based practice such as "how am I experiencing this moment of being alive (HAIETMOBA)" or "What is this?", "Where is the self?", etc.

As I said, I'm not a very rigorous formal meditator—a lot of this stuff I see on walks, exercising, etc. as well as sitting in meditation.

Hope this helps!

Elena: What is "I" for you?

Peter: I would start with the living body—no living body, no me. Therefore me = body.

Elena: Really? Or are you just throwing out propositions? Do you truly believe you are the body?

I am not going into any discussions with you. You are the one who needs to look. So if you believe you are the body—then look closer. Which part of the body is you? Exactly which part?

If not, then try to cut each part of the body and see what remains. Can you find "you" there?

Go.

Peter: No other way to communicate than with language, concepts. Can't upload my experience to you.

OK—if I look, I can't see "self as body". Looking and experiencing the self are incompatible activities. If I look, all I experience is looking. So maybe the self is "my unique perspective when I look".

But of course I can't look at my perspective. So I could say from that point of view that my perspective doesn't exist. Or I could say that it's like a fly on the back of my head—something that exists but can't be viewed directly.

Elena: If your family's life depended on how honestly you were looking at reality, you would not give concepts. You would communicate, hard. Yes, it would be expressed in concepts—but the focus would be on finding the truth, on getting it across.

So stop just throwing ideas out, and look.

The "unique perception when you look" is part of reality, "you" is not. You do not exist. "You" is a thought of "you". Thought exists. You do not.

Find out if this is true. Take the time. Find out. And that's not to say perspective isn't unique—unique perspective exists. But who OWNS that unique perception? That perception? That uniqueness?

Who? Find out. Dig. Investigate, hard, do it now, and don't stop till you find the truth.

Peter: I look and I see phenomena—no self there.

However, I also see behaviour that seems to imply a self—in the way that praying seems to imply the existence of God.

When I was a kid and started to doubt the existence of God, praying seemed like a waste of time and I stopped. But the equivalent behaviour that I see in myself—I'll call it "selfing"—it seems like it just carries on whether I believe in it or not.

Elena: Nice. So if the prayer stops, God as a thought will disappear, but God as Existence itself won't, right?

Same here. If you stop a behaviour, change a behaviour etc., the self doesn't have anything to do with it. It's just a thought, a label. Existence itself is selfing as all these unique embodiments.

Can you see that Life is just life-ing? There was never you there, an object. All this time, if we apply time, all what was happening is life lifting, patterning as "Peter", 'you'.

See if you can find a unicorn in your room. If I tell you this, you won't even try to find it—you know it does not exist. Why would you look and look for a self that is the same—a thought, a label?

Look deeper. Tell me what you see.

Peter: What I see today is: nothing different between inside and outside. Just matter interacting with matter. So nothing special about the inside part.

And that made me think—is this like being a robot? A robot is no different from the stuff he's made from—there's nothing "extra". If he has a sense of self. that's just a program running.

But then I thought—no, a robot is still a kind of a thing that is separate from his environment, his context. But if the inside is the same as the outside, there's really no way to differentiate—there's no basis for that separation. So no robot.

All these words and labels (not just the "self" ones but perhaps all of them)—maybe they don't mean anything at all. I think I'm seeing that they are just patterns being exchanged back and forth, like birdsong. There's this pattern of back and forth and somehow we get a self from that.

I see that sensation is very mysterious. How does it just happen on its own? Why is it happening over here and not over there? I'm not looking for answers, just noticing that this is something very strange.

Elena: Just beware of focusing on examining concepts in your investigation. Examine reality. Inside-outside is something that you heard, and now you are trying to fit the reality into the concept. You did right with the robot, but it's more deductive reasoning than looking at reality.

The birdsong thing—yes, that's good. Dig into that more. I like that.

But to say "There's this pattern of back and forth and somehow we get a self from that."—No, there is no self. No. No. No. Who is this "we" that gets a self?

You see it? The label arises from thought, but it doesn't point to anything. Is that true? Find out.

As for why sensations are happening over here, and not over there—who cares? It's a red herring, refocus, don't get distracted. Instead, ask—and find out—where are they coming from? Where are they GOING TO? Are they coming from a self? Are they going to a self? Are they?

Sensations are part of reality. They exist. Just like flesh, thought, feeling—all part of reality. Existence. You have no trouble noticing a sensation or feeling or thought.

So why it is hard to notice the self? Why it is so vague, illusive? You can't pinpoint it just like you can do with sensation, thought or a cup on your table.

Find the answers to these questions.

Peter: OK, so what I get when I look now is a sense of inversion—of the current flowing in the opposite direction from before. I'm reminded of an album title by a band I like—"And then nothing turned itself inside out".

Elena: Look at your immediate experience and write again. Is there a "you" in reality?

Peter: Work is a bit busy. Looking out the window there is light, movement, etc. In the body there is warmth, sensation, etc. A sense of continuity from one to the other. No ownership or causation as such. That's about it.

Same feeling as yesterday that something is reversed from how it used to be—tough to describe more clearly than that. It feels good, though.

Elena: Ok perfect. No ownership. And what is "I"?

Peter: There's no answer to that question—the word "I" has no referent that is real.

Elena: Nice—good—but it sounds a little like you're parroting. Get into more detail, more depth. Dig. Find out if this is real, and how it is real, and the contours of that reality. Right? That's something that goes totally beyond agreement, it's a whole different level, it's exploration.

Peter: No problem with that.

So, taking a look at the light on the trees outside the window.... Now as we've discussed, there is, in the act of looking, no experience of the looker, nothing except the totality of looking.

And because there is no looker, there is no experience of past or future either, because these things are just ways of referencing the looker. And there are a bunch of other things that are just no longer relevant for the same reason.

So there's an experience of a lot of what you might call "suffering" being out of the picture because it really has nowhere to grab onto in this sense of just being.

So this is way better and truer than the old behaviour that has been reinforced since childhood—which seems quite bizarre from the point of view of just being. More than that—it seems actually painful to contemplate the idea of "selfing" and all it involves: things like guilt, shame, worry.

Elena: Great, great.

Define "self", please. What is "self"? What is "I"?

Anyone living life?

Peter: Well, 'selfing' is a behaviour really. Mainly a verbal/cognitive/discursive type of behaviour, so it's based in language. So from that point of view, "I" is a word. However, that doesn't mean it points to anything that exists.

I guess you can have a label that has nothing existing behind, it in the same way you can write a check with no money in the bank. The behaviour is not supported by ontology.

So any "one" living life? No, the living of life happens as experience only. It's an impersonal process. There's an experiencing of that process, but the experiencing is not compatible with owning it or identifying with it.

Elena: is there a "you" in any shape or form in reality?

Peter: No!

Elena: Ahahahaha! Is it kind of like a joke?! Tell me, dear friend, how are you doing?!

Peter: Yes—no "me"—it's strange. Everything is different but the same. No big fancy words to describe it. No words at all in fact. But it's freeing, that's for sure.

Elena: Yep. Look at it like this—Life was there before, and self was never there. "Self" was just a concept, thoughts, a mental construct. So Life was always living without self, so to speak. And Life is "life-ing" now. So what's changed for Life? Nothing. That's why it is so plain, so simple, so ordinary. But so fascinating how it was not seen!

So no big bang, you didn't become a saint or an angel.

You became natural. That's all it is. A free man—an embodiment free of self-concept.

Of course, years of self-preservation created a lot of tensions/resistances/limiting beliefs in the body/mind. It takes some time to unfold those "tension pockets".

This was awesome, Peter. I really appreciate how you stepped up. And if you remember how vague you were in the beginning, look at the clarity and simplicity of what was realised.

Thank you very much for liberating consciousness—each time there is a relaxation in the embodiment, ripples of that go and touch others, if we can put it in this imperfect wording. That is why it is so easy now to wake up—it's a wave, a tsunami.

Much love! Warmly hugging you.

Peter: Hugs in return! Clarity and simplicity, yes... I've waited a day to reply just to see what happened. Of course everything is still the same—there's nothing else to happen really. Thank you, Elena for all your work, this has been truly helpful.

Garsius

Garsius was getting it on an intellectual level; all that was left was seeing it clearly. It did not take him long to realise that "I" is just a label and emptiness is not personal. I was really happy to help Garsius, as he comes from the same country as me. I did not reveal it till afterwards; it was a big surprise for him.—I. C.

Ilona: Hi, Garsius.

How are things looking today?

Garsius: Hey.

Today is a lazy day. I'm doing nothing and there are many ideas around—I should do this, do that, just not to be still, just not to be... Most of those ideas are seen and witnessed. Some missed. Anyway, this day is beautiful.

As I look now, there is a shift, where "I" goes from "doer" to "doer and witness of doing". That shift happens very often, sometimes a few times per minute. There is a big need to dig more into spiritual things, like reading Elena's blog or watching an online satsang. Holding off from this as Elena suggested.

Anyway, as I write those "I", "me" etc., there is an understanding that here is no "I", just thoughts arising. Problem is: that understanding is intellectual, like one more additional thought about "no me".

Ilona: I see. OK, if you get it intellectually, great. Let's get you to really seeing this. Where do thoughts come from?

Garsius: From an empty area in the middle of my chest.

Ilona: Can you control them?

Garsius: Nope.

Ilona: Do you know what the next thought is going to be?

Garsius: Sometimes. There is some kind of knowing of what thought will come soon given the circumstances around me. Hard to describe. No sense in that.

Ilona: What influences thoughts?

Garsius: A thought comes when the time and place are right for it to come. It's like when the same thing happens, the same suitable thought will arise. And if you're conscious of that, it may happen again and again.

Ilona: Can a thought be stopped in the middle?

Garsius: Yes, seems so. If you become conscious of that thought, it stops in the middle. But either way, I know what that second part would be.

Ilona: Have a look at thought itself and write what you see.

Garsius: Thought arises from empty space, generates one feeling or another in the body and disappears. Sometimes I can be so still as to watch and fully realise that. Thought is not me. Seems like "I" should be the one who watches thought.

Ilona: OK, let's look at this more closely. Notice that thoughts are just labels and that the mind is a labelling machine. Sensation arises and thought follows, sound is heard and a label follows. Look around the room, notice things and how the mind labels them automatically.

Garsius: Yes. That can be seen easily. That doesn't happen for all objects, but for many. For example, I look at a picture with a sunflower on it and the thought arises: "sunflower". Actually, it is a picture not a flower, isn't it?

Ilona: Next look at labels themselves. Some words point to real things. Some point to symbols and imaginary stuff.

Garsius: Yes. And that cannot be controlled—it happens automatically. If you try to force looking without labelling, even then it's replacing a label thought with one dead empty thought, or something like that.

Ilona: Look at the word "table" and see the table in front of you. You can touch it; it's real.

Take the word "university". Is there a university in reality? There are buildings, people, desks, computers, books, but no such thing as university. So it's a label that we use so we can communicate about it; but there is no such thing.

Examine the label "I". What does it point to? Anything real?

Garsius: It points to the complex of body, thought and feeling. Is it real? I struggle here.

Ilona: How about Santa?

Garsius: There is no Santa, only ideas about him.

Ilona: How about self?

Garsius: Nope there is no self. Only the idea that this body and thought complex is me.

Ilona: Cool, let's look at that "I" thought together.

"I" points to thoughts about "me", but there is no "me" in there. Check—is there a "me" in the body other the thought of "me"?

Garsius: There is no "me" inside except that thought about "me". Then "me" wants to hang on as the observer who observes the "I" thought and all other stuff inside and outside.

Ilona: The word "body" points to the body, "thought" points to thought, "feeling" to feeling. Real stuff.

"I" points to thoughts about "me", but there is no "me" in there. Check—is there a "me" in the body other the thought of "me"?

What breathes? Is it you breathing or the body itself?

Is there a breather?

Is there a walker or is walking happening?

Is there a digester? Or is digestion happening?

Is there a feeler?

A thinker?

A witness?

A drinker?

An eater?

Garsius: It happens by itself. I can just be aware of it or not. Who is aware, then? Yeah, I can see that awareness happens by itself too... Who is aware of awareness then? Damn, that is confusing...

Ilona: See where I'm going with this?

"I" is just a label that is used for communication so we can understand language. But "I" is just a label and not a doer.

Awareness just is. Does it need an "I" to be aware?

Garsius: No, no need for an "I" to be aware.

Ilona: Do you have a pet? Look at any animal, see how it is aware of environment. But is there an "I" that is aware?

How about a fly? A bird? Is there a manager in there that is aware, or is awareness aware of itself by itself?

Garsius: Animal eyes are empty. There is no "I".

Ilona: Any observer? There is observing happening, observed, observer and observation being one process. Is there a separate being that is observing?

Check that.

Look at how everything is happening by itself. Thought comes up, fingers type, words appear on the screen. Is there an observer outside this action happening?

What is being noticed? Is there a noticer?

Garsius: That emptiness is aware of thoughts. Thoughts arise in that emptiness and end there. So that means I'm emptiness?

Seems like that observer, that awareness is localised in the body somehow. All is observed from the body point.

Ilona: What is being noticed? Is there a noticer?

Garsius: Emptiness is a noticer.

Ilona: "That emptiness is aware of thoughts. Thoughts arise in that emptiness and end there. So that means I'm emptiness?"

No, that does not mean that you are emptiness. It means that emptiness is, but there is no you at all. As in zero.

Is this true?

Garsius: I don't know.

No. Honestly I know: there is no "me".

Still this feeling of "I" is here. Yes, a huge label of "me".

Grrr, I want to get rid of that labelling...

Ilona: Labelling is happening and there is no one here to get rid of it. It's happening and it will be as it always was.

It's not the labelling that drops and not the feeling of beingness, but the belief that there is a "you" to which all this is happening.

And that drops because you see the truth that actually, in real life, there really isn't. So investigate that first and foremost.

Life is. You aren't.

Do the math.

Garsius: There is a feeling of apathy here. It's like "yeah, yeah, that is true, but—whatever". Sometimes moments of strange happiness come, then everything's the same again.

Ilona: Good, good, it's all happening. There is no "you" to see but seeing is happening. Is this true?

Garsius: Yes, it's true—there is no "me" seeing, just a feeling that it is "I" who sees, seeing happening by itself.

Ilona: The feeling that it is "I" that sees—look there. There is a feeling of seeing + labelling. = "I see". Look at that feeling again. Get on it, don't be shy. Climb inside it, look at the world from that perspective.

Seeing is happening....

Ilona: How is everything looking today?

Garsius: Peaceful, quiet and no one cares even about such nice things. Today there is no apathy. Today is... nothing.

Ilona: How does it feel to be liberated?

Garsius: Like a beginning, or something like that. There is a strong need to show this to others also. There is silent gratitude with no target for it. And mind becomes like this: "oh, I should be very happy" and disappears. And there is love—silent warmth towards all: you, Elena, table, rain...

Ilona: Awesome! Thank you. Much appreciation here.

There are some questions left that we need to go through just to clarify, but I see you've made it.

Answer when ready.

Is there a "you", at all, anywhere, in any way, shape or form?

Garsius: Nope, there is no "me" at all.

Ilona: Explain in detail what the self is and how it works.

Garsius: I don't know how it works. Somehow "I" is connected to every thought that comes. That is how "I am that, I am this, I feel this, I don't feel that" is here. Somehow there is a belief about that—that you are this every statement "I am...".

Like you are inside thought. You are content of that thought and acting with no questioning. If a question arises, it becomes an "I" immediately. So that, Ilona, the nonsense of self goes on forever.

Ilona: How does it feel to be liberated?

Garsius: It's just perceiving all happening, looking at the "I" thought without being touched by it. Actually, you are not touched by anything. There is no "you". Nothing. Everything. But not "I". Even "I" is in that everything.

Ilona: How would you describe it to somebody who has never heard about "no you"?

Garsius: Spontaneously.

There is no "you". Look and see that there is the body, thoughts, feelings etc., same as other things around in the world. Perception of those things happens, but there is no perceiver. The "I" thought is everywhere, but it is not you. Try and find that out yourself.

Anything you can identify yourself with while trying will be false. You can't be the thing you're looking at. Look and take off layer after layer of that false "I" until nothing is left of "you".

Ilona: Brilliant!

The last bit: is there any doubt at all?

Garsius: Nope, there is no doubt. "I" can return, but it is always clear that it is not me.

Ilona: Perfect. Can you tell me what pushed you over? What was most instrumental, what made you actually look? Can you look back and see if you can pinpoint that shift?

Garsius: Cannot say. Maybe that will come later. You and Elena just chopped, chopped and chopped. And somehow, at some point some resistance fall apart and nothing was left... Hah, now tears come. Much Love here.

This morning, when I opened my eyes, there was full clarity. Later I slipped and again did not understand what and how. (There was understanding, but also a thought that I don't understand anything.)

There was nothing left to identify with, not even with emptiness. After this apathy started, like "oh well, it does not matter" and later something gave up. There was nowhere to retreat. Seeing happened.

Thank you.

Greg

Greg is a very serious Theravada Buddhism practitioner. With him, I challenged his most basic spiritual beliefs: why meditate, cause and effect, karma—those that just come with classical meditation path in a package, and are not usually doubted. But pondering them made him see the truth.—E. N.

Greg: Hi, Elena.

My name is Greg. My friend Shane recommended I talk to you, and I do have a question about my practice that is ripe for help and guidance.

I hope you don't mind spending some time on this with me. I'll give a brief overview of where I'm at, but I just wanted to make sure you are open to it in the first place.

Elena: Hi, Greg. Yes. Perfect timing. Please write anything you want me to know.

Greg: Thanks so much for volunteering your time for this! The last couple weeks have been very interesting indeed. On the night of Friday the 26th of August, Dominic, whom I think (hope) you have spoken to, gave a talk in which he announced that he no longer has a self.

During the course of that talk, I witnessed a swing between deep scepticism to sweet, promising confidence. Scepticism because nothing that was said was foreign here, yet I had not knowingly shed my self. Promising confidence because the allure of "if Dominic is free and I've had the same experiences, then I might be free." After all others had left, Dominic and I spoke for several more hours.

He asked me questions such as "what is the 'I'?" and "who is Greg?" Although I had my own abstract understanding of answers for those questions, I did not have any formulated for an actual face-to-face inquiry. It seemed so ridiculous to be faced with such a question.

Internally it was something like, "What is Greg? There is no Greg, come on that's obvious! Why do I have to put this in words?" I did formulate some answers using words like illusion, veil, and even "misconception that hijacks experience". It was all quite unexpected. I can remember a time gone by that my answer would have been much different. What had changed and when had it changed?

The days that followed that night were full of unsettling confusion, contemplation and uncompromising investigation. Now the confusion has been burned away. Please feel free to contradict the conclusions that are offered. Even the harshest assessment of delusion is welcome.

There is no Greg to get upset, only a process of mental and physical phenomena that this mind once attributed to a self. And yet, there is still the behaviour as if there is a Greg!

This is where the confusion took hold. What had been shed and what was still there? Now, it is understood that the belief that "there is a Greg, a persistent core that is at the heart of all experience here" is gone, probably for the remainder of life. However, all of the structure the supported that belief for 33 years, the habitual behaviours, the deeply memorised patterns of action, even the unspoken compulsive self-centric thoughts, persist.

Prior to Tuesday the 30th, that distinction was not understood, and so the direction for practice was somewhat wayward. Now, the distinction is clear and it seems that there is a defined direction to progress. The "I" that is the reflection of a lifetime of "I" must be undone.

So begins this slow, steady practice of unconditioning the behaviour of "I". Is this correct? Is there a faster or more direct way? Or a better, less confrontational way? As far as I can tell, each time a conditioned behaviour that once supported "I" arises, all that can be done is to recognise it for what it is, make mental note that there is no "I" so the behaviour is outmoded, and wait for the next one to arise.

Sometimes it happens that thoughts arise without "I" as the centre, whereas before "I" was always the centre. For instance, the words might effortlessly arise as "there is hunger" instead of "I am hungry".

Other times, it's "I am hungry" followed by "what? What 'I'?" Still other times it's more like, "I'm hungry" and then … hell, just be lazy. I'm prepared to progress in this way, yet it seems somewhat tedious.

Open to anything you are willing to offer. Many thanks!

Elena: Why do you meditate?

Greg: I meditate to bring some "not doing" awareness into this life.

Elena: So you and life are separate? You need to do something to bring something to the life that already is?

Greg: Not at all, not sure where you get that. How can I and life be separate? The very idea is preposterous.

There isn't a single shred of evidence that there is an "I" to be separate. Furthermore, true separation in this universe is impossible, it is only illusory separation that people invent.

Elena: This is just intellectual talk. You're spouting dogma, theory. You have to get real, get looking, get investigating. That alone can deliver freedom.

Greg: If the mind has its way all the time, active and unbridled, then it is spoiled just as a child that gets everything it wants.

Elena: And you think you are changing something here? There is no you.

Greg: Cause and effect. Whether there is "I" or not is irrelevant.

Elena: There is no cause and effect. Not really. It's something the mind layers over the flow of things. And when humans look at life through a causal lens, the idea of the 'self' is the result.

Greg: There are many great benefits to meditation, some known here by experience, others by passage of information. Nevertheless, right now it all seems to boil down to just opening some space for pure awareness.

Elena: What? There is ONLY pure awareness. No opening is necessary. Look deeper. Anything is outside the pure awareness? Anything? Anything at all? What? Mind? Conditioning? Anything outside?

No more opening needed.

Need to just see that what you want to open already is. No "you".

Greg: It's true that it cannot be shown that there is anything outside awareness. Yet that does not prove that ALL there is is awareness. How do you jump to that conclusion? Looking deeper indeed.

Elena: I am not proving anything to you.

You need to see it for yourself. Who is there to be liberated?

Greg: Who is liberated? I (please overlook the convention of speech) know only how it feels to no longer believe in an "I" . All feelings are exactly as they were when there was belief in "I". But then, there never was an "I" in the first place, so why should they be different?

The body is slightly nervous at being questioned. Mmm-hmm! Useless conditioned response.

Elena: So what is that what you want?

Greg.

Greg! It's not a conversation. What I am asking you or writing to you has nothing to do with logic, knowledge or intellect. You don't need to prove anything to me. I don't need to prove anything to you. You wrote to me. Why? What is that you want?

What are you still looking for?

What are you trying to find?

WHAT IS NOT YET HERE?

Greg: What I want is the end of my suffering. When I say "my", I know that it is not actually "my" suffering. Still, it seems like there is suffering temporarily, and at those temporary times it seems like there is a "me" to experience the suffering. Then the suffering evaporates and the sense that "I" felt it goes away too. Perhaps this is only intellectual understanding.

Elena: How do you see the end of suffering?

Greg: What am I trying to find? I guess it would be help with looking deeper.

Elena: Why do you need that? What is the drive behind it? Look, break it down, what is there?

Greg: What is not here yet? I have no good answer for this. At least when I calm down and am quiet, I don't seem to perceive that anything is missing.

Elena: So when you are not calm and quiet, is there anything missing?

Greg: Hi, Elena, I took a little time to wait for "not calm and quiet" so that I could answer your question. It's not happening, though, so I'll address your questions now anyway.

"How do you see the end of suffering?"

Good question. I suppose my ideal is some long-lasting fantastic mind state that is not reactive to anything. At least that is what my idea of the end of suffering has been for so long.

As I was writing my last message to you, I realised I am now confused about suffering where I was once clear about it. It used to seem so solid and I could say "yes, there is suffering, how to find a way out!" Now though, it's difficult for me to say it with certainty.

I know there is no self and this knowing is present now under conditions that would have caused me definite suffering before.

When I am feeling something unpleasant and even the mind makes an unpleasant reaction, what used to be suffering is more like... just the unpleasant thing and then just the unpleasant mental reaction and maybe even an unpleasant physical reaction to the mental reaction. And then they all fade and I'm a bit confused.

Did I suffer just then? I think it used to be suffering, now not sure. It looks more like just stuff happening and "unpleasant" is a part of it. Was the "unpleasant" suffering? How can it have been? It was just the unpleasant whatever. Then where was the suffering? Was the unpleasant mental reaction the suffering?

I used to think so, oh yes! But now I pause there and look. It doesn't look any different than the "unpleasant" in the first place. Just another "unpleasant" with a different flavour, but soon gone. Then where was the suffering in that? Seriously! I've seen suffering before, where did it go?

I'm sorry to go on, it's just strange to be confused about this now and it's hard to express the confusion. How can I find the certain end of suffering if I can't even find the suffering for certain? It doesn't make any sense at all.

What am I trying to find?

"I guess it would be help with looking deeper."

"Why do you need that? What is the drive behind it? Look, break it down, what is there?"

Good question again. When I first felt the need to ask for help, I was extremely disturbed. And then this shift in understanding happened and I wasn't confused at all anymore.

So just as Shane gave me your details and suggested I ask you for help, the gripping desperate need for it vanished. Ah-ha, so finally I answer the question. I don't need it. But I didn't see any harm in completing the original intention to contact you.

At least when I calm down and am quiet, I don't seem to perceive that anything is missing.

Whoa! I tried to answer "what is missing" three times, decided my last answer was good, headed for bed, and then suddenly this 1 + 1 = HOLY SHIT happened!

Every time something seems to be missing, the thought that perceives the missing thing always has an "I" in it!

If there is unhappiness, it's just unhappiness. But if I am unhappy, "I" need to be happy; happy is missing! If uncertainty pushes to the top, there is great uncertainty. But when I am uncertain, I need to know; knowing is missing! What the fuck! Can't believe I didn't see that happening before! Before "I", nothing is missing. Only "I" makes it missing.

How totally awesome! Wow, there is a LOT there. So much to watch.... too excited for bed. Heeheehee.

Elena: Absolutely amazing! Greg, well done! Awesome! Now answer me some questions:

Did you ever exist?

Can you find "you" in any shape or form in reality?

What is "I"?

Greg: Hi, Elena, sorry about not replying sooner, how did five days rush by so fast? Thank you for asking some fun questions.

As funny as it sounds (it still sounds really funny over here), I must conclude that I do not exist and I never existed. The reason I must conclude that is precisely because I cannot be found in any shape or form in this experienced reality.

Furthermore, I cannot find anybody to dispute this statement with any meaningful evidence. The only thing that is found, in looking longer and deeper for the Me that is promised by thought, is the absence of "I" wherever the search is directed.

So what does this mean?

That "I" never existed is not to say that nothing exists, nor is it to say that Greg doesn't exist. What it is saying is that Greg as perceived by the thinking mind does not exist.

That Greg is only imaginary, a fabrication of mind that is no more real than the details of a memory. True, conditions that give rise to a memory are real, but the content of the memory is not. In the same way, the content of the mental image, the promise of Greg is not real. Because the content of that mental image of Greg was promised to be real and to exist, and that content is now known to be illusory, it can be said that Greg does not exist. The promise was empty.

"I" is an idea in the head, a mental concept, and that is all. So "I" only exists in so far as the idea exists. To carry on from here represents too much opportunity to over-think the question and thinking is what created the illusion of "I" in the first place.

These are some questions that have already come from others. If "I" don't exist, what is left? This is the part I really love. It doesn't matter. Arguing the deeper implications would just be a mental exercise rife with opportunity for the illusion of self to continue.

"I" is unreal, so what's after "I" a is waste of energy. Indeed, the need for "after I" is just more "I". Where does "I" go? Perhaps "POOF" is a good answer. The opportunity in every moment is to exist in that moment, not separate from it in any way. What could be more important than that?

Ok, historical ramble mode on here. The Buddha characterised four stages of enlightenment. Penetrating the illusion of self was one of the factors of the first stage, along with lack of need for rites and rituals, and the eradication of doubt.

However, it was said that total liberation is still not achieved due to the persistence of the most subtle forms of self-conceit. I think I remember one form of that conceit being the desire to live or die, something like that.

As someone who hit the first mark, I intend to keep practising as before by observing non-self both directly and indirectly. If there is a point here, it's that the self conditioning began further back than accessible memory recalls.

Since old memories are triggered out of the blue by certain conditions the resemble those at their origin, it follows that echoes of self may be deeply buried until such time as conditions support their lapse. If they do arise, then a new awareness will be present to meet them. How cool!

Elena, thank you soooo much. Tremendous love and appreciation for you here.

Just so awesome! Frequent laughter over here for absolutely no reason, it's just a delight and it's awesome!

Please don't stop helping others. What a gift!

Caroline

Caroline came very ready. There was some sadness, and we worked through that. After this she only needed a little push and then she started laughing. She was looking for something else, something big and magical, just like everybody else, so when she saw the reality of it, it brought up giggles. It was a beautiful transformation, from sadness to love and gratitude. Nice and simple.—I. C.

Caroline: Hi Ilona! Thank you for taking the time to speak with me. Feeling excited like a little girl and a little tired too. But YES, I want to go all the way through. Before, I thought I had to get prepared, to know, so that I could succeed at what you would ask me. Now, I feel that the best is to not know. So yes, let's go for it. And I'm willing to be honest.

Love.

Ilona: Awesome. So tell me. As you see it now, what is "me"? What is self? What is "I"? Just answer as you see it.

Caroline: "Me", "self" and "I" are thoughts.

Ilona: What do they point to?

Caroline: Nothing. Now it comes too: "self", "I" and "me" point to nothing as thoughts.

Ilona: Where do thoughts come from? Can you control them? Can you stop one in the middle?

Notice how the thoughts "I" and "me" just come and go like other thoughts. Can a thought think?

Caroline: I can't find where they come from. No, I can't control them. No, I can't stop one in the middle.

Yes, yes, yes, "I" and "me" are the same as other thoughts. Oh my. So much energy through the fingers. No, a thought can't think.

Ilona: So if I say that there is no self at all in real life, is it true? What comes up? Check your feelings.

Caroline: Woke up this morning with intense contraction in the upper chest. Seemed like self is that. Then saw that it's just a thought arising about this feeling. As if the thought is "this contraction shouldn't be there".

When reading you now, I seemed focused on this sensation, as if yes, there is self and it's located here. Writing this, there is relief now.

There is no self in real life. Feelings happen like the feeling of contraction in the upper chest. Thoughts happen too, like "self is the contraction in the upper chest, "contraction in the upper chest shouldn't be there"... Just thoughts.

I notice sadness now. Often felt that when focusing on "no self"... some thoughts arising like "what am I going to lose?" Yes, just thoughts. "I can't let go of taking myself for these thoughts, contractions." "What is going to happen?" There is labelling of the contraction in the upper chest. And there is a kind of attachment that it's me.

Let me send you that.

Ilona: Yes, thoughts feelings just come and go.

Notice how well they are connected—thought triggers feeling, feeling gets labelled, that again triggers feeling and then it's rolling.

But can you look at the feeling itself, notice where it feels, bring it closer and honour it? Say "sadness, please come closer. I feel you. What can you show me? I respect you and bow to you."

Then see what is behind sadness. Is there anyone that sadness is happening to or is it just a feeling that came for a visit?

Let me know what you find.

Caroline: Yes, Ilona. Thank you. Let's carry on.

Thank you so much for what you said about how to address the feeling. It didn't work straight away... There was contraction, wanting to escape. The belief in failure was triggered too. So yes, I noticed how it's rolling like you said.

Then I tried to ask "sadness" if it likes being sadness. And it answered "no" and asked me to liberate it. From this moment I began to feel profound relaxation. I wanted to say "I love you" to sadness. It lost its grip. It felt like I'm the love the contraction is looking for.

Or it could be more accurate to say that love is always here. Can't find anyone or anything that could be love. This appeared weird to the mind but I felt the impulse to surrender to how the response to the contraction was appearing. And it was all very subtle.

But I couldn't deny the feeling of profound relaxation, warmth and love. Then a feeling that appeared stronger than sadness appeared as doubt. It took more time to lose its grip. But now it seems that it did. Other feelings arose again too, like failure.

What is behind sadness? Only thought. No, sadness happens to no one. Yes, it just appeared.

Felt the impulse to check now what comes if I say: "there is no self at all in real life." Yes, it's true. Now there is a feeling of joy in the upper chest, like wanting to laugh instead of the contraction, sadness, doubt. I mean, feelings still appear, but it doesn't happen to a someone.

Before, it felt like I wanted to get rid of the mind's functioning, wanted to get rid of labelling, feelings... Now it seems like it doesn't matter, as it's not happening to someone. And at the same time, it seems that the contracted parts that are still looking for something are noticed more than before. And the response as the feeling of the loving presence happens too, spontaneously.

So now it seems that stillness is always here somehow, whatever arises. There is nothing to hold on to. And at the same time, even if doubt cannot stay or mean anything, noticing thoughts like "this cannot be it, this cannot be liberation, it's too simple." And the response appears as a subtle laughter, no excitement, nothing special. I mean I always imagined that I will feel something special. Like a beautiful story of how "me", "I", disappeared. ~laughter~

Seeing that "I" as reality has never existed... ~laughter~ But I was looking for something other than This. ~smile~ What is there now doesn't look like anything I have ever imagined. There was seeing before that appeared like this but now I see that there was someone in control of the seeing too. This is incredible. Feeling like energy is liberated in the shoulders, feeling heat. Seeing the belief in being Caroline as a construct, nothing real… OMG...

Let me send you this. Your help is very appreciated. There can be something hidden I'm not seeing. (There is a feeling of tiredness now that may show something too.)

Ilona: Wowowow! I'm delighted for you.

Yes! This is great. I love the bit about laughter. Isn't that just ridiculously funny? And you understood how to deal with feelings.

I have some questions left for you.

1) Is there a "you", at all, anywhere, in any way, shape or form?
2) Explain in detail what the self is and how it works.
3) How does it feel to be liberated?
4) How would you describe it to somebody who has never heard about no you.
5) What is real?

Caroline: Perfect. ~smile~ Everything just as it is. Beautiful sunny day in Paris, in awe with the breeze in my bamboos. Feeling lazy, still.

Yes, let me answer the last questions.

Aahahaha.. This first question is making me laugh again.

I felt the impulse several times to answer this question in a funny way. But then the thought came: "no, answer this in a serious way".

Can't help it. So here is the answer: and I say no, no, nonono. No. No. there's no me at all. Aahahaa. There is no me at all anywhere, in any way, shape or form.

The self is a total construct, a belief in a separate entity. It works with identification with memory, thoughts, sensations; identification with the "I" thought.

How does it feel to be liberated?— ~smile~ This question triggered tension so many times. It feels wonderful to see everything as it is. Nothing needs to be different. It feels like everything is traceless. It just happens. fresh. Thoughts happen, labelling happens and yet it cannot define what is. Isn't this wonderful?

Yes, this body-mind mechanism is just amazing. All these words, labelling, cannot stop. There is a kind of laziness to answer the questions, first. And yet, words come, there is joy and I'm amazed by that.

"How would you describe it to somebody who has never heard about 'no you'?"

Everything just happens and it happens to no one. No one is doing anything. Doing happens. Thoughts, sensations happen. But no one is doing all this. (not sure I would say that to my grandma but who knows. ~smile~)

"What is real?"

This moment as it is. Seeing, typing, feeling.

Well, that's it. Don't see anything else to say for now.

Thank you.

Ilona: BEAUTIFUL. Yes, the shift has happened for sure. Now it's a matter of settling in.

Wow.

I am amazed that you did it so quickly. Thank you.

We also have a group that offers aftercare. Everyone in there has seen though the illusion and it really helps, when stuff comes up, to talk to others. I'll add you there, just adjust the settings. Stay around for a bit. It really helps.

Love you!

Caroline: Tears arising, Ilona... They arose yesterday too, with immense gratitude for you. I can't explain this feeling.

I am amazed too. Maybe one can say the path had already been clear enough. Needed a little push. And life beautifully guided me to Elena's blog. And from then I began to feel something within was feeling seriously in danger. Then read your blog. Such deep resistance, fear of dying, feeling of lack, of lacking liberation, to "it doesn't matter at all. I'm fine."

When I read some folks criticising you and Elena, I could so relate. I had the same thoughts, same critiques. But something kept showing me that I was lying to myself in resisting. And yes, humility seemed to be asked for. But now it is seen as nothing.

I knew I couldn't continue to live a lie anymore, as subtle as it may appear. At the same time, the resistances were arising, there was such wonder about what I felt was going on with what I felt you and Elena were offering. It reflects so much all the unknown about what is going on on this planet. I was sceptical about you and Elena.

You know, it's like we hold on so much to the past, to the old ways, like pretending to know how liberation should look like. Anyway, I trust that, like I experienced, resistance will have its time, but one day or another we'll be unable to not answer the call.

Yes, felt touched by reading the "falling" part today. And I am so grateful that you and the other friends are here to support me. I have found this nowhere else. This is so precious. And all this without asking for money. Hmmm. Heart filled with deep gratitude.

I am already in a group where I wasn't supposed to be. Ha! But anyway, it helped to be in this group before seeing through the illusion. Seeing that it works and being inspired by others' honesty did help for sure. I saw your post about another group too today. Wonderful. Feel inspired to help too.

Even before seeing through the illusion, it was there. But it was obvious that I couldn't help others see what I didn't see myself. I trust life to guide me perfectly here. Feel the need for things to settle more too.

I love you too, my beautiful friend. How grateful I am for trusting you. Like you say, things get interesting in "falling". Let's see what comes.

Ilona: Thank you. Lots of appreciation here. Lots of love.

I have been so busy with organising our new playground at Liberation Unleashed, and it's going to be grand. When it settles you are welcome to join in to help others.

For now, rest, Caroline. It's like being reborn and none of the old makes sense any more, and the new is not settled yet. Just trust in the process, and if anything ever arises that you want to talk to me about, I'm here for you.

Much love.

Gratitude and Appreciation

This book could not have been produced without the team of amazing individuals involved in its creation.

Our deepest thanks to everyone who participated in these conversations. Thank you for sharing your journey. In so doing you are reaching out to help those who are still searching. Many people have reported that the shift happened for them while reading our blogs; we hope this book will spread the message even further, reaching every person who may benefit from it.

We thank all those who worked on this book, helping with editing, design, and advice. Thank you Chandi Riaz, Ciaran Healy, Alexei Stephenson, Viv Westbrook, Jeff Montgomery, Matthew Brown, Diego Stargazer, Bonnie Aungle, and Nona Parry for making this happen. Additional thanks to Damon Kamda and to Tina Huebner Patlyek for administrative assistance during the project.

Ilona and Elena

6509676R00133

Printed in Great Britain
by Amazon.co.uk, Ltd.,
Marston Gate.